Nahid Persson Sarvestani

Visionaries: Thinking Through Female Filmmakers
Series Editors Lucy Bolton and Richard Rushton

Title in the series include:

The Cinema of Marguerite Duras: Multisensoriality and Female Subjectivity
Michelle Royer

Ana Kokkinos: An Oeuvre of Outsiders
Kelly McWilliam

Gillian Armstrong: Popular, Sensual & Ethical Cinema
Julia Erhart

Kathleen Collins: The Black Essai Film
Geetha Ramanathan

The Cinema of Mia Hansen-Løve: Candour and Vulnerability
Kate Ince

Céline Sciamma: Portraits
Emma Wilson

Shirley Clarke: Thinking Through Movement
Karen Pearlman

Habiba Djahnine: Memory Bearer
Sheila Petty

Marleen Gorris: Practices of Resistance
Sue Thornham

Nahid Persson Sarvestani: Towards A Liquid Authorship
Boel Ulfsdotter

Nahid Persson Sarvestani

Towards a Liquid Authorship

Boel Ulfsdotter

EDINBURGH
University Press

Edinburgh University Press is one of the leading university presses in the UK. Publishing new research in the arts and humanities, EUP connects people and ideas to inspire creative thinking, open new perspectives and shape the world we live in. For more information, visit www.edinburghuniversitypress.com.

We are committed to making research available to a wide audience and are pleased to be publishing Platinum Open Access ebook editions of titles in this series.

© Boel Ulfsdotter, 2025, under a Creative Commons Attribution-NonCommercial licence

Grateful acknowledgement is made to the sources listed in the List of Illustrations for permission to reproduce material previously published elsewhere. Every effort has been made to trace the copyright holders, but if any have been inadvertently overlooked, the publisher will be pleased to make the necessary arrangements at the first opportunity.

Edinburgh University Press Ltd
13 Infirmary Street, Edinburgh EH1 1LT

Typeset in 12/14 Arno and Myriad by
IDSUK (DataConnection) Ltd

A CIP record for this book is available from the British Library

ISBN 978 1 4744 7987 5 (hardback)
ISBN 978 1 4744 7988 2 (paperback)
ISBN 978 1 4744 7989 9 (webready PDF)
ISBN 978 1 4744 7990 5 (epub)

The right of Boel Ulfsdotter to be identified as the author of this work has been asserted in accordance with the Copyright, Designs and Patents Act 1988, and the Copyright and Related Rights Regulations 2003 (SI No. 2498).

EU Authorised Representative:
Easy Access System Europe
Mustamäe tee 50, 10621 Tallinn, Estonia
gpsr.requests@easproject.com

Contents

List of figures   vii
Acknowledgements   viii

Introduction   1

PART ONE: Prostitution and polygamy: two close-ups of patriarchy   41

1. *Not* accented cinema: *Prostitution Behind the Veil* (2004)   44
2. Hegemonic patriarchy and polygamy: *Four Wives, One Man* (2007)   53

Conclusion to Part One   60

PART TWO: New narrative and formal interventions   65

3. Auteurism in accented cinema mode: *The Queen and I* (2008)   71
4. First signs of collective authorship: *My Stolen Revolution* (2013)   85

Conclusion to Part Two   101

PART THREE: Authorial divestiture in the twenty-first century   107

5. Expanding her documentary apparatus: *Be My Voice* (2021)   113

6. Polyvocal political activism as a matrix for the liquid
   documentary: *Son of a Mullah* (2023)   125
Conclusion to Part Three   138

Summing up   140

References   160
Filmographies   164
Index   166

Figures

Figure 1.1	Fariba with her son waiting for a suitable customer, *Prostitution Behind the Veil*. Screenshot by author.	46
Figure 1.2	Mina and Fariba share a large room in a squalid former townhouse, *Prostitution Behind the Veil*. Screenshot by author.	49
Figure 2.1	One wife's story in *Four Wives, One Man*. Screenshot by author.	58
Figure 2.2	Family picnic in *Four Wives, One Man*. Screenshot by author.	60
Figure 3.1	*The Queen and I*. Screenshot by author.	79
Figure 4.1	Pantomime in *My Stolen Revolution*. Screenshots by author.	99
Figure 5.1	*Mise-en-abîme* in a secondary frame in *Be My Voice*. Screenshot by author.	122
Figure 6.1	The director as investigative journalist in *Son of a Mullah*. Screenshot by author.	130
Figure 6.2	Narrative interval in *Son of a Mullah*. Screenshot by author.	135

Acknowledgements

This book has been several years in the writing and even longer on my mind, mainly due to scholarly delays caused by the Covid-19 pandemic. I am therefore very grateful for the continued support of my editor, Gillian Leslie, and the series editors (Lucy Bolton and Richard Rushton), and for their immediate embrace of the slightly altered framing of the book's subject matter. On the positive side, the volume's overlong gestation somewhat unexpectedly offered me the opportunity to include two more films by Nahid Persson Sarvestani in my survey of her career as a documentary filmmaker.

During the writing period I have also had generous economic support from the Lauritzen Foundation, which has made it possible for me to present and discuss my work at several international conferences. The foundation has also supported my research trips to archives such as Women Make Movies (WMM) in New York, thereby allowing me to accrue material which has contributed significantly to my study of Persson Sarvestani's documentary practice. Thank you very much indeed for your continued support of my research.

I would also like to express my gratitude to all of the staff at the film archives and libraries for their diligent assistance during my, at times, challenging research.

Last, but not least, I wish to express my heartfelt gratitude to my husband, Mats Björkin, for his unwavering support and encouragement of my scholarly endeavours. They could not have come about without him.

Boel Ulfsdotter, November 2024

For my mother, Barbro, the painter and cineaste who first introduced me to the ways of seeing.

Introduction

In *Prostitution Behind the Veil* (2004), the Swedish Iranian filmmaker Nahid Persson Sarvestani shares the distressing story of two women, Mina and Fariba, who had never lived with men who were not violent towards them or their children. They now had to sell their bodies to strangers as both had become addicted to heroin through their former husbands. The film is a straightforward social documentary for television. But it is also a film with delicate ethical and artistic considerations. Here is Sarvestani's own account of making the film:

> It happened many times during the shooting that I turned the camera off and went to comfort Mina's and Fariba's children. I have cut out the scenes where the women abuse them from the finished film, although I realize that these incidents were ample proof of the mothers' horrendous despair, and I am never afraid to tell the truth. But it was too awful. I was afraid the audiences – with their limited knowledge of their overall life situation – would not offer these women the empathy that they were after all so worthy of. (Persson Sarvestani 2011: 258–259, my translation)

In *Prostitution Behind the Veil*, we see the early traits that have made Persson Sarvestani such an important filmmaker. She takes an intrepid, vocal approach (*Prostitution Behind the Veil* won the Golden Nymph Award at the 2005 Monte-Carlo Television Festival for Best News Documentary). Her concern is for the women whose lives she wants the world to know about:

women in Iran, which she herself left in 1982, soon after the Islamic revolution. Her involvement with and commitment to individuals, communities and events is expressed cinematically in the film which, by choice and by necessity, includes key issues within the Iranian diaspora.

The documentary practice of Nahid Persson Sarvestani now spans three decades. With the exception of *Son of a Mullah* (2023), all her political documentaries have focused on Iranian women's history and present living conditions after the Islamic revolution in the late 1970s. Their activist purpose and wide international recognition have been fulfilled through festival screenings and continuous availability through replay services provided by, for instance, Swedish Television.

In terms of her film practice, I argue that it has taken unexpected turns over the years, not only because she became persona non grata in Iran after making *Prostitution Behind the Veil* (2004) and *Four Wives, One Man* (2007) in situ in the early 2000s. Her focus on Iranian women's continuous hardships persisted, and it consequently forced her to reinvent her practice and explore other documentary strategies to express her political and feminist activism. Generally speaking, these circumstances have resulted in three thematic documentaries and three documentary portraits.

Nahid Persson Sarvestani in brief

The Swedish asylum system did not differentiate between whether it was religion or politics that had driven a certain individual to flee Iran in the 1980s, given the atrocities the Shah's security police had committed against civilians before the government was toppled. In view of the Iranian diasporan community's size and rapid formation in Sweden, and the extremely high level of education of its nationals, Iranians were quickly integrated into Swedish society. Hence, Persson Sarvestani did not have any difficulty finding work related to the country's recent history when she embarked on a career as a filming TV journalist, later moving on to become a politically dedicated documentarist.

After her arrival in Sweden in 1982, Persson Sarvestani soon went into formal training to become 'a proper journalist' (Persson Sarvestani 2011: 213). The critical stance held by the exiled Iranian community had by then hardened and was more or less entirely focused on the social and juridical atrocities the Islamist regime carried out, not least the wiping out of all women's rights and the enforcement of veiled dress. In view of these political developments, Persson Sarvestani began her media career on a voluntary basis, working on the production and broadcasting of radio programmes in the Persian language at the local radio station in her hometown of Uppsala. She found herself utterly taken by the medium and its affordances and decided on a career in media. After working with the editorial staff at the local radio station, she took several community-sponsored courses on video production for televised broadcasting. She started filming her kids and their friends at pre-school as an independent filmmaker for practice. Persson Sarvestani then went on to take different types of commissioned projects, mainly information films, until the early 1990s, when she started working more regularly with the editorial staff producing *Mosaik* – a social issues programme targeting immigrants in Sweden, broadcast by Swedish Television (SVT) between 1987 and 2003. Established in the 1950s, Sweden's national broadcaster copied its basic form from the British BBC Television. SVT began making news documentaries about developing country topics in the 1960s in connection with the war in Vietnam, which meant that social issues programmes like *Mosaik* were in a TV format which was already well known to Swedish audiences (Persson Sarvestani 2011: 241–245).

As a Swedish documentarist of Iranian descent, Persson Sarvestani has presented work based on feminist representations that inform international audiences about the effects of the reinstated patriarchal rule in post-revolutionary Iran. Recent work in this area includes Jeff Kaufman's film *Nasrin* (Kaufman, 2020) about the Iranian human rights activist and political prisoner Nasrin

Sotoudeh. In this book, I argue that Nahid Persson Sarvestani's documentaries should not be seen as feminist interventions based on her transition to living in Europe for two obvious reasons, the first being that her interest in women's issues was already part of her professional and political agenda already during her early attempts at journalism in Iran shortly before the revolution in 1979. The second reason is that Persson Sarvestani did not receive formal training or work as a proper journalist until she settled in Sweden and started her professional career in the late 1980s.

However, her interest in issues pertaining to politics, democracy and gendered equality in post-revolutionary Iran has remained central to her journalistic and documentary practice throughout her professional career. This has widened the gap between her practice and Hamid Naficy's matrix for the production of 'accented cinema', as we shall see below (Naficy 2001).

It thus seems to me that Nahid Persson Sarvestani's career development reflects a will to set aside the Romantic notion of professional prestige in favour of an exploration of the joint affordances offered by a more pronounced transmedial documentary process. Her documentary practice is allowed to continuously reflect on complicated, important events in politics and feminist history as a result of her authorial dedication to any new discursive tenets related to the documentary process itself. Together with a pronounced search for an intersubjective relationship between filmmaker, subject and spectator to maximise the films' reception, I claim that these two trends (evolving subject matter and formal preoccupations) are representative of Nahid Persson Sarvestani's move towards liquid authorship.

Consequently, this book studies the shift in Persson Sarvestani's documentary practice over a period of 20 years (2004–2023) framed within three main topics:

- the progression of her applied documentary modes;
- her documentary apparatus in relation to the development of online documentary media;

- her documentary editing strategies employed to address and narrativise women's life experiences in particular.

Early films

Persson Sarvestani writes of her professional career in Sweden that by the mid-1990s, 'I was increasingly pleased to express myself through the film medium' (Persson Sarvestani 2011: 247). Her self-motivating realisation, and the way she readily introduces herself as the enunciator of her films, is the starting point of my study of her documentaries on different aspects of post-revolutionary Iran.

As an example of her journalistic approach, Persson Sarvestani writes in her memoir that she filmed everything she saw when she revisited her birthplace, Shiraz, for the first time in 1999. 'During the six weeks I spent in the country, [I saw quite enough] of an Iranian society in disarray for my anger from the revolutionary days [in my youth] to be rekindled' (Persson Sarvestani 2011: 250, my translation). 'Aside from the obvious signs of poverty and suffering, I also noted the small but uncanny changes of people's mind maps, for example regarding veiling' (Persson Sarvestani 2011: 251, my translation). Although Persson Sarvestani was indeed already well versed in political theory when she left Iran as a young woman, her comments seem to confirm the embedded potential of her intellectual double-bind in that she was 'influenced by a European gaze and interest, as well as an insider's gaze and knowledge' (Van de Peer 2018: 56). In my view, this intellectual double-bind has been conditional to her success as a politically invested documentary filmmaker.

None of this, however, appeared in Nahid Persson Sarvestani's first documentary feature film, *Seventeen Years of Longing* (Persson Sarvestani, 1999), which was sponsored by her then employer Swedish Television. 'Accented' notions that invoke escapism or limbo remind us that the film's overall *sujet* indeed matches a film category that Hamid Naficy has designated as clearly nostalgic and complementary of Iran. Adding to the film's air of open-hearted happiness to be back in the homeland is perhaps the general optimism invoked by the Islamist regime's gradual move towards increasing openness in the late 1990s under then President Mohammad Khatami's rule (1997–2005). Discussing diasporan filmmaking in this mode, Naficy points out that the production of Iranian 'accented' feature films has generally been more profilic and reached a more widespread audience in the United States. The European exiled communities have remained or become more acutely invested in political counter-narratives, a direction which is confirmed by Persson Sarvestani's documentary practice (Naficy 2001: 77).

Shortly after the release of *Seventeen Years of Longing*, Persson Sarvestani again returned to Iranian subject matter in her second documentary, *My Mother, A Persian Princess* (Persson Sarvestani, 2000). After being contacted by a young Swedish photographer named Anna S., the director decided to produce a film about her under her own label, Reel Films. In this 48-minute documentary Persson Sarvestani accompanies Anna S. on her return to Iran to see her biological mother for the first time. The spectator finds herself *in medias res* without further ado, with the narrative beginning in a Swedish shop selling fully covering clothes for orthodox Muslim women. In terms of background, Anna S. begins to tell her story in short sequences using voice-over accompanied by footage from everyday life in her small apartment. Persson Sarvestani assists her during telephone calls to her mother in Iran and on her visit to the Iranian embassy to get a visa. The film fabric does not reflect any signs of overt authorial directorship, nor is there a strong sense of enunciation given that Persson Sarvestani does not take part in the voice-over commentary. This means that she appears as more of a sidekick than film director in this production.

Once in Iran, Anna S. gets to meet her entire biological family, and later confirms in voice-over that she found the situation extremely confusing, emotionally draining and difficult, as she knew nothing of Iranian culture and could not speak with them directly. Following these comments, again made after her return to Sweden, Anna S. also criticises the society she sees outside her Iranian family's house in terms of women's hardship under the veil and the unmasked female subordinance in society. One of the examples she offers is the fact that women are forced to sit at the back of buses, while the men take in the fresh air at the front. Anna also comments on the billboards with the faces of religious clerics towering over the cityscape, which is again confirmed in the visuals from the filmed footage.

During all these events the exact interchanges between Anna S., Persson Sarvestani and Anna S.'s family are not related through subtitles for the onlooker. Sadly, the director's translations to Anna S. have been edited out as well. This discursive oversight comes across as even more unfortunate when a completely unforeseen turn of events occurs when Anna S. visits the orphanage where she lived from the age of six months until she was adopted by her Swedish parents at the age of four. On this occasion, the onlooker is only indirectly made aware that contrary to Anna S.'s biological mother's earlier statements about how she was forced to give her child up for adoption, the head of the orphanage claims that her mother never once visited Anna S. before she left Iran for Sweden. The camera is then directed towards her biological mother as she, in apparent embarrassment, again tries to explain herself. Because no translation is given, the onlooker only learns about these facts when Anna S. airs her huge disappointment and emotional shock in her later voice-over comments. She makes the decision to still go ahead with her plan to go and see her biological maternal aunt and, judging from the filmed footage, that seems to have been a happy reunion. Soon afterwards, however, Anna S. decides to cut her visit short and brings forward her return flight from Iran to Sweden by several weeks. The film ends with footage from her apartment in Sweden and Anna's voice-over comments about her enormous disappointment towards her biological mother, and how she felt much closer to her siblings and her aunt. She confesses to deep feelings of relief at being back home, before the film abruptly ends followed by the closing titles.

As I have already suggested, *My Mother, A Persian Princess* is in many ways lacking as a documentary film product. The absence of complete subtitles indicate that it was primarily made for an Iranian audience and not intended for international theatrical distribution. Formally speaking, the cinematic presentation reflects an overall observational documentary mode composed of unsentimental images, although the unsynchronised editing sometimes blurs the narrative components. In terms of its shooting, this documentary engaged no less than three film photographers, leaving Persson Sarvestani fully inscribed in the filmed footage as Anna's guide and translator throughout. The visuals seem to be edited in a basically chronological order but do not always match the statements made by Anna S. in the later voice-over commentary.

The director's continuous interaction with the documentary subject was key, as Anna did not speak Persian or have any prior experience of Iran or the Iranian society. After brief opening credits, the spectator immediately lands in the clothes store where Nahid Persson Sarvestani is advising Anna on appropriate clothes for the trip. There is no introduction to the film's topic on tape by either of them, so we must presume that this film was aired as a news documentary for an Iranian television audience and introduced by the programme's host. Persson Sarvestani confirms this hypothesis in her memoir, where she writes that the film was made for the community programme *Mosaik* (Persson Sarvestani 2011: 254). The major sequences involving conversations or monologues in Persian without subtitles risk coming across as insignificant to an outsider watching the film, especially undermining the unexpected turn of events at the orphanage when Anna S. learns that her mother never visited her or objected to her being adopted by her Swedish parents. Did her biological mother in fact sell her to the orphanage? Not being able to understand what the personnel is saying – nor her mother's response – when these facts are unveiled leaves the viewer unnerved, but this also leads to a lack of empathy for Anna S. when she later confirms in a voice-over how deeply this emotional betrayal affected her.

The film offers no closure for either Anna S. or her biological mother. What remains is an impression of Anna S.'s implicit critique of her mother's failure to mother her, as well as her own critical comments about Iranian society in general, and women's hardship in particular.

I put forward that the reason for the lack of epistolary clarity in the current version of *My Mother, A Persian Princess* is mainly due to its remaining unsatisfactory editing. Whether a narrative closure would have been feasible with a more careful editing process we do not know, as it would have depended in part on the availability of relevant original footage. The film is now too quickly paced, which obscures the information it seeks to convey.

As previously mentioned, one explanation for its cinematic disposition could be that it was framed by either a spoken introduction by the programme's host or a group discussion in tandem with its original broadcasting on *Mosaik*. The omission of subtitles indicates that in either case, it was targeted at a select audience. These original production conditions aside, the only explanation as to why it has been available for streaming is that its inherent critique is still made quite clear.

From the point of view of Persson Sarvestani's future career as a feminist documentarist, the interaction with the young woman in this early film bears no sign of the extent to which their shared observations had fuelled Persson Sarvestani's anger at the societal state of Iran at this point (the beginning of the twenty-first century), nor does she give away that the post-revolutionary elimination of women's rights will actually become the main topic of her future documentaries. In her memoir, Persson Sarvestani writes that although she put on a big smile during both visits that formed the background for her first two news documentaries, her fist was clenched in her pocket, and she was ready to start researching material for a more openly critical film about Iranian society (Persson Sarvestani 2011: 254).

Contemporary women Iranian filmmakers

I here use the word 'contemporary' to introduce women Iranian filmmakers that have documented Iranian women's situation, from inside and/or outside the country, during the same period as Nahid Persson Sarvestani, which is to say roughly since the beginning of the twenty-first century. In terms of general film history, Iran has a longstanding tradition of popular cinema production, which resulted in a booming national film industry from the 1940s until the Islamic revolution in 1978–1979. The post-revolutionary era has seen more women filmmakers come to the fore in all genres in tandem with the regime's effort to generally increase the artistic quality of Iranian cinema. In terms of the country's documentary cinema tradition, this group of women filmmakers has split into two groups. The first group is tolerated by the regime and is thus allowed to both work and exhibit their films inter/nationally. The other group is barred from both producing and screening works pertaining to Iranian subject matter inside the country, thus practising mainly outside Iran.

The catalogue of Women Make Movies, a non-profit distributor of independent films by and about women, reveals that films on Iranian women's lives or living conditions have mainly been produced by filmmakers working outside Iran.

Examining the archive of recent documentary films on this topic, Reza Poudeh in 2010 introduced the genre as follows:

> Documentary filmmaking flourished in Iran during the 1950s and 1960s (one of the best known is Forugh Farrokhzad's 1962 documentary *The House Is Black*). Among the top documentaries produced in Iran in 2007–8, five were by women. Recent documentaries in Iran tend to be well-researched and make use of various styles. (Poudeh 2010: 411)

Poudeh then goes on to reference the narratives of five films, including Nahid Persson Sarvestani's documentary feature *Four Wives, One Man* of which he wrote: 'The film's success in capturing life in the raw, with its many riveting scenes, makes it an excellent way of exploring the social and psychological implication[s] of polygamy' (Poudeh 2010: 413). What is more interesting is that this review essay does not include a conclusion of any kind. It leaves the reader with short final remarks on each film, like the one cited above. The author thus abstains from any qualified opinion on female Iranian filmmakers producing documentaries on Iranian subject matter from abroad, despite the fact that Poudeh himself has produced numerous documentaries and short films on 16 mm film and video.

In what follows, I briefly introduce a few fellow filmmakers whose work on female subjectivity, or their own working conditions, is thematically connected to that of Persson Sarvestani.

A few years before Persson Sarvestani released her first documentary on Iranian subject matter, *Prostitution Behind the Veil*, Mahnaz Afzali had shot *The Ladies' Room* (2003). It is a documentary about Iranian women of all ages visiting a public restroom in a park in major Iranian city, perhaps Tehran. The choice of locale for this film production is interesting for two reasons; first, it is an enclosed and 'neutral' space. Second, although a ladies' room nominally draws visitors from all social strata, this particular restroom is situated in a public park, which has a decisive impact on its clientele. The women who come here talk to the woman overseeing the restroom and returning clientele about rape, prostitution, addiction, incest, police violence, harassment, mental instability, even suicide. Although their life stories do not explicitly address political issues, nor religion, each story tells us something important about the society they live in. The onlooker quickly concludes that these are extremely vulnerable women, most of them homeless, which normally calls for a respectful and considerate documentary approach through the observational mode by the documentarist. Afzali, however, proceeds in an expository manner with intrusive close-ups, verbal encouragement reeking of bias, and prying questions, such as 'Are you still prostituting yourself?', 'What do the johns look like?', 'Show me that scar again!'. The film is edited to present individual segments of a group of women, resulting in an organic and fluid narrative of their precarious living conditions. *The Ladies' Room* is thus thematically akin to Persson Sarvestani's *Prostitution Behind the Veil*, but the difference in documentary modes indicates the former filmmaker's complete lack of empathy with the women's situation compared to the Swedish production.

Twenty years later, Majed Naesi's documentary *Inside the Iranian Uprising* (Great Britain, 2023) reflects a less stigmatised and more rebellious attitude among mainly Iranian youths. The main topics addressed in this documentary resembles those addressed by Persson Sarvestani in her documentary portrait of Masih Alinejad in *Be My Voice* (2021) but differs from it in two important points. First, Naesi's film *comments on* rather than investigates the events at hand. Second, *Inside the Iranian Uprising* begins with the death of Mahsa Amini in September 2022, which means that it takes over where Persson Sarvestani's documentary left off.

The film's first segment is dedicated to the widely circulated official footage of the Iranian police abusing and severely injuring Amini, and how it started an unprecedented riot among young Iranians. Taking place mainly online, the demonstrators share abuse videos and other forms of witness documentation showing, for instance, female police officers swearing to kill all female protesters. According to the voice-over in Naesi's documentary, hundreds of women were arrested for the same reason as Masa Amini was, which is to say for not being properly veiled. The segment goes on to present the Women Life Freedom movement, which emerged in response to Amini's murder, including footage of young Iranians (both men and women) cutting off their hair in protest. As a means of emphasising the societal shift on women's issues instilled by the Islamist regime, Naesi next inserted archival footage from the era of the Shah regime, demonstrating women's substantial contribution to society, and especially the workforce, at the time. The Iranian women's immediate awareness of the new regime's ensuing change in attitude towards them is documented in archival footage of demonstrations that took place in the early 1980s.

The second segment of *Inside the Iranian Uprising* consequently deals with the authority's crackdown on the young protesters, which started immediately after Amini's funeral. It is composed of reiterated footage of activist protests posted online, documenting their vast unrest and calls for gender equality, but also mothers' witnessing about their daughters' suspicious deaths at the hands of the morality police. One of the more well-known cases also in the West concerns 'Nika', who was arrested during the protests. Her social media accounts were deleted, but her family was still denied any news of her situation – all the while she was already dead, having committed suicide by supposedly falling from a high building, according to the police. The footage from the funeral shows a banner saying 'Happy martyrdom, Nika!' which indicates the level of self-sacrifice among Generation Z Iranians today. According to the voice-over narrative of Naesi's documentary, the Iranian police force has been instructed to confront the rioters severely and seriously since Nahiri's death. This order has also led to the arrests of journalists, the confiscation of documentary material, internet blackouts, and officials closing down private social media accounts or ordering individuals to close their accounts and delete footage. Citizen surveillance is extensive and aided by informers.

In terms of the documentary practice framing *Inside the Iranian Uprising*, the film consists of compiled media footage from the internet in combination with an explicatory voice-over narrative. This means that, unlike Persson Sarvestani, Naesi does not investigate or contribute to the film's content but only comments on it. Her approach is therefore more in line with traditional feature-length TV reportage and prevents it from being labelled as an original documentary production. My assumption is confirmed by the tone of voice used in the voice-over guiding the onlooker through the material, as it closely resembles that which you hear in daily news broadcasts. This particular film characteristic at the same time also confirms that *Inside the Iranian Uprising* was intended for a uniquely Western audience.

Other contemporary film productions are aimed primarily at the Iranian diaspora, such as Tania Amadi's film festival dedicated to women filmmakers in Iran, organised and screened digitally from New York in 2021. The rich and varied programme contains a list of documentaries on various topics ranging from rice farming in *Mother of the Earth* by Mahnaz Afzali (Iran, 2017), to children's schooling, to films on political topics, like *Our Times* by Rakshan Bani-Etemad (Iran, 2002), as well as the internationally screened *Formerly Youth Square* by Mina Akbari (Iran, 2019). The latter is introduced as follows:

> Journalist Mina Akbari's FORMERLY YOUTH SQUARE, which opens with a photograph of a group of 70 journalists taken about 20 years ago in Javanan Square. Of those, only six continue to work in their profession, including the filmmaker. Many emigrated after the 2009 unrest that followed allegedly rigged elections, a few were imprisoned, and other simply left the field. Akbari narrates the film and interviews many of the journalist from the shuttered Jame'e newspaper. They speak about repression and their professional histories, referring to the difficulties and pitfalls of their careers in Iran. Formerly Youth Square drew such a large audience because such sensitive topics are rarely discussed in public forums and because the filmmaker is herself a respected journalist. (Programme presentation, Iranian Women's Film Festival 2021, *sic*)

Mina Akbari, who is now based in London, is currently completing her new documentary with the working title *Women of the Revolution*, produced during an internship at Wissenschaftskolleg zu Berlin. The following project presentation is on their website:

> 'Women of the Revolution' shed[s] light on the adverse effects of the discriminatory and oppressive laws enacted by women members of the Iranian parliament. Thus, the documentary investigates the struggles of women in reclaiming their lost rights after the Islamic Revolution. It features interviews with women representatives of different periods in the Legislative Assembly of the Islamic Republic, giving their reactions to the oppression of women. In addition, the film tells the story of my life from the age of two, when the Islamic Revolution took place in Iran, up until I turned 46. It recounts my experience of being summoned to the morality police for the crime of not wearing a hijab

while driving in my car. This documentary is in the final stages of editing, and I plan to complete post-production while at the Wissenschaftskolleg (Mina Akbari, 2023)

Unlike Nahid Persson Sarvestani, Mina Akbari is still permitted to film in Iran and is therefore able to base her films mainly on documentary footage shot in the country. Contrary to Persson Sarvestani's documentaries, Akbari's films may still be legally exhibited to Iranian audiences.

There is also Mania Akbari, whose work has been screened widely in the West since the early 2000s, including at international film festivals. Using film as her primary medium of communication Mania Akbari started out as an artist, exhibiting video art and installation work, seemingly sharing a certain artistic affinity with another Iranian screen artist in exile, Shirin Neshat. Already considered controversial in Iran, Akbari recently released *How Dare You Have Such a Rubbish Wish* (2022), which in my view is a scantily cloaked, and thus ingeniously devised, political allegory. It is a compilation film, based entirely on excerpts from so-called 'film farsi', a popular film genre 'famous for its preponderance of images depicting sex, crime, and the lowly cabaret', which was quickly banned as vulgar by the Islamists after the revolution in 1978–1979 (Fish 2020: 53). Instead of disappearing from view, however, this film genre has resurfaced in remixed versions which, according to Laura Fish, are 'driven by a productive form of nostalgia' (Fish 2020: 54). In Mania Akbari's hands, the soft-porn aesthetics of the prolific scenes of women's singing and dancing in abandon to Iranian males have been very cleverly compiled into short clips, which ends up making the informed female onlooker almost nauseous with *discomfort* rather than feeling nostalgia. I therefore suggest that the strongly demarcated excerpted scenes, including the editing of shots depicting the interaction between male and female characters in these scenes, result in a twofold political allegory. The first variable constitutes the well-known reminder of women's ingrained submission to the tradition of pleasing the patriarchal gaze. A more unexpected outcome is the reaction that the continuous inclusion of the filmic representation of the observing male character/s instils in the onlooker. It seems to me that instead of stopping after the exhibition of the female acts (in pursuit of nostalgia), the accompanying footage of the male characters' reactions to the women's displays of intellectual, sexual and performative submission brings home the actual problem with ingrained patriarchal and misogynistic values. These male characters are presented as perfectly dimwitted because they are haunted by such outrageous lust! In view of our non-agitated, sublimated views on women, sexuality and soft porn today, it seems that Akbari's counter-narrative in *How Dare You Have Such a Rubbish Wish* is thus primarily aimed at unveiling the ridiculous, laughable male characters, perhaps even asking if this was the actual reason for the film genre being banned by Iran's new regime.

The most well-known contemporary women Iranian filmmaker is probably Shirin Neshat, a world-famous video artist and filmmaker who has received several awards for her films. In 2009, Neshat directed her first feature film, *Women Without Men*, which introduced her focus on the problematics of the female body, and how it continues to be a contested space for sin, shame, violence, repression yet rebellion, power and protest under patriarchy. Her 2023 exhibition *The Fury* included a video installation which, in a highly fictionalised and stylised manner, addresses the sexual assault of female political prisoners subjected to severe torture. Even after being released, many of the women are unable to recover emotionally from the trauma experienced in prison. The video traces the psychological and emotional journey of a young Iranian woman, who, although she now lives freely in the United States, remains traumatised by the memories from her time in captivity.

In summing up, Mania Akbari's filmmaking, like that of Shirin Neshat, is directed towards implicitly unveiling post-revolutionary Iran's continuous blatant female repression. However, these directors have opted for counter-narratives with a less directly political agenda than that shown in Nahid Persson Sarvestani's documentaries. Before I move on to the films, there are cultural markers that need to be addressed to fully appreciate my positioning of Nahid Persson Sarvestani's political documentaries.

Geopolitical and culture theoretical framework

Although Iran's film industry should formally be included among the developing country cinema nations, it must be remembered that the country itself was never victim to colonisation. Its film industry was thriving before the Islamic revolution and has also continued to release award-winning fiction films of high quality after 1979. Iran's escape from traditional colonialism means that in this book I dispense with a clear-cut post-colonial theory referring to the colonial gaze, studied for instance by Ella Shohat, G. S. Spivak and Ch. T. Mohanty.

However, Iran was never *governed* like a Western-style democracy either, given that its last monarch, Mohammad Reza Pahlavi (1919–1980), identified as an authoritarian leader on the topic in all interviews currently available on internet. As mentioned earlier, Iranian women at the time still had extensive societal rights to, for instance, undertake higher education programmes, have a professional career, vote, marry who they wanted and divorce. Polygamy was not allowed, and women were legal subjects with shared responsibilities/rights for their children's upbringing. Iranian women could be seen in society without male chaperones and were allowed to dress as they saw fit. Veiling was optional and left to each woman's individual choice. A certain form of patriarchy still prevailed in twentieth-century Iranian society, but men and clerics had no direct power over women's daily lives. The religious revolution and subsequent installation of the Islamic republic in 1979 abolished most of these rights for women and made them subject to complete patriarchal rule (see, for example, Wikipedia). The discursive tenets of patriarchy in combination with those of twentieth-century feminism is, however, not at the immediate centre of the theoretical discussions about Nahid Persson Sarvestani's career as a documentarist in this book, as already stated above.

Iranian women's history in brief

Writing on Iranian women's home videos, Lidia Merás offers a succinct summing up of the initial radical change in Iranian society in 1979. As is already a well-known fact, '[t]he 1979 Revolution was initially a popular uprising supported by a heterogeneous amalgam of Marxists, nationalist, Islamist and other disaffected groups that opposed Mohammad Reza Pahleví's authoritarian regime and its feared SAVAK national police force' (Merás 2018: 182n). The political situation, however, changed dramatically '[o]nce Khomeini came to power, disenchantment soon followed among secular sympathisers. Left militants and other dissident groups (e.g. Kurds) were tortured, killed or incarcerated' (Merás 2018: 182n).

Looking back at women's history in Iran, Tania Ahmadi asserts that 'the feminist movement in Iran and Iranian women's quest for equal rights and sociopolitical empowerment date back to the late nineteenth and early twentieth centuries, when newly formed modern social movements began to strive toward constitutionalism and a democratic nation-state' (Ahmadi 2023: n.p.). This is an important statement because it shows that Iranian women have worked for gender equality for the same length of time as women in the West: '[t]he first women's associations, usually semi-secret, helped promote women's literacy; demanded women's access to public education, hygiene, and vocational training; and criticized women's seclusion, marital polygamy, and domestic violence' (Ahmadi 2023: n.p.). These rights were extended to women during the Shah era. Women's legal rights were equal to men's at the time, polygamy was not allowed nor was *sighe* (see below), and women had full access to all levels of society (see, for example, Wikipedia). 'With the swift rise of Islamism after the establishment of the Islamic Republic as a theocratic state in 1979, many of the laws and policies in both the public and domestic domains came under the direct control of the clerics, who extended gender discrimination in favor of men' (Ahmadi 2023: n.p.). I thus hold that it is indeed possible to apply the tenets framing the Western feminist movement to my discussion of the post-revolutionary events related to Iranian women's issues in this book.

Once the establishment of the Islamic Republic in Iran got underway in 1979, the bulk of Iranian refugees arriving in Sweden were intellectuals or people from higher education programmes such as medicine and engineering, but also religious nationalists. Others were members of the Iranian student unions who had demonstrated against the country's former monarchic rule, in favour of a modern democracy. Nahid Persson Sarvestani was one of them. Arriving in Sweden on a false passport in 1982, she has become Sweden's most accomplished political documentarist.

The veil

Listening to Anna S.'s comments about how she is sweating in her head scarf in *My Mother, A Persian Princess* gives the onlooker an idea of what it is like to wear clothes that cover your body from head to toe. And yet, she is not wearing all-black outfits like many Iranian women do. The opaque fabrics of course make them even hotter, which suggests that this enforced dress practice is socially self-censoring in the sense that women hesitate to go out and confront the scorching sun.

The tradition of the veil suggests that it saves women from unknown men's gaze or touch. According to some, it does not, however, acknowledge the fact that this type of covering makes women more vulnerable at all levels of society. From a feminist point of view, the tradition of veiling women and the idea that it signals their modesty outside the home disregards the symbolic fact that a veil like the hijab in effect makes women invisible to the surrounding society. They become a non-entity, which makes patriarchal domination so much easier, both socially and juridically. Women may only unveil themselves at home and can disregard wearing the veil when in the company of male family members inside their house. The discriminating treatment of women also includes a gendered segregation of space hindering women from entering certain areas, even in their own homes through the same door as the men in the family.

Because it is now a mandatory dress practice, the symbolic and political implications of the veil tradition are visible to a higher or lesser degree in all of Persson Sarvestani's films. Its existence and display in Middle Eastern culture and political ideology has remained stable, although ideologically incoherent, for hundreds of years. According to Leila Ahmed its modern trajectory in Iran began with Qassim Amin's publication of *The Liberation of the Woman* aka *Tahrir Al-Mar'a* in 1899, in which he announced that Arab women should adandon wearing the veil in favour of a more Westernised dress. To Ahmed this change in dress practice, however, mainly reflects Amin's willingness to take on board the views held by Western colonisers, thus uttering that the veil was representative of developing countries' general 'backwardness' and their urgent need for civilisation to become more palatable to the West: 'Well-meaning European feminists ... earnestly inducted young Muslim women into the European understanding of the meaning of the veil and the need to cast it off as the essential first step in the struggle of female liberation' (Ahmed 2003: 47). Their intentions, however, misfired, according to Ahmed (ibid.), as the veil came to be a means of resistance to Western imperialism, whether colonial or post-colonial.

Although different leaders of Muslim societies navigated towards a Western cultural and societal affiliation, including in Iran, they nevertheless continued their efforts to use dress reform as a vehicle for social reform. Reza Shah Pahlavi (1878–1944) went as far as banning the veil, whereas his son, Mohammad Reza Pahlavi, the last Shah of Iran, decided to make wearing the veil optional. With the Islamic revolution the veil again became a mandatory item of clothing for Iranian women, although the practice of exactly how to wear the veil, or shador or hijab, was not a pivotal topic of discussion until Mahsa Amini was arrested for unlawful dressing in 2022 and died due to physical violence while in police custody. The continuous and prominent visual appearance and problematisation of the veil in Persson Sarvestani's films hence regained momentum as a political (leftist) signifier pointing towards a non-patriarchal, secular society based on gender equality, ruled without any interference from religious groups, regardless of religious affiliation.

With regard to the cultural and sartorial politics of the veil, it is important to point out that women in other Muslim countries and societies, from Egypt to Indonesia, have established different views on this clothing item. Besides its religious significance, the varying functions and values of veiling may entail, for instance, a notion of empowerment by women who choose to wear it as a way of removing their bodies from male scrutiny and social judgement. Defiance in relation to utterances of Islamism and other forms of patriarchal or religious fundamentalism therefore cannot be automatically linked to Muslim women's sartorial tradition of veiling. Abdus Sabur, for instance, asserts that 'emerging middle-class Muslim women encounter challenges when they position themselves through veiling as a strategy aiming at class recognition and preserving relative status' (2022: 401). One of the reasons for this conduct, according to Sabur, is that these women are facing 'an accountability structure—a system of monitoring and assessment to enforce normative expectation[s]—which leads them to engage in veiling' (Sabur, ibid.).

From a historical point of view, Malika Boussoualim outlines the changing cultural and gendered history of the debates about veiling in Algeria during the twentieth century, highlighting its effects on women. Boussoualim claims that 'since colonial intervention with veiling, Algerian women's bodies have often triggered controversies affecting women's lives negatively' (Boussoualim 2021: 1291). She concludes that

> while veiling is getting mystified and stripped of meaning under much manipulation through denigration or glorification, women's lives are affected in different ways by the polemical debates. The most tangible effect is the violence endured by women because of the growing tensions between the two sides of the debate. (Boussoualim, ibid.)

To fully understand the discursive implications of the early visual history of women and the veil in Iranian society, Hamid Naficy's inscription of the so-called averted look and direct gaze in post-revolutionary Iranian fiction film history is helpful. The 'Islamic' averted look prevents people from looking directly at others, based on differences such as class, hierarchy and gender. A person can also be scrutinised with a direct gaze, which is averted when they return the look (Naficy 2003: 141).

Immediately after the revolution, all images of unveiled women were cut from existing Iranian and imported films in an overt act of censorship and falsification of (film) history as well as women's history. Female subjectivity was also largely excised from new local productions, forcing directors to refocus their professional interests on either war films or films for children. During the second phase of the revolutionary aftermath, in the mid-1980s, this act of censorship led to

> women appear[ing] in local productions either as ghostly presences in the background or as domesticated subjects in the home. They were rarely the bearers of the story or plot. An aesthetics and grammar of vision and veiling based on gender segregation developed, which governed the characters' location, dress, posture, behaviour, voice and gaze. (Naficy 2003: 144)

The third phase of post-revolutionary filmmaking appeared gradually and saw a more dramatic presence of women both in front of and behind the film camera. With it came a certain liberalisation of modesty rules, according to Naficy, leading to an increasingly more convincing treatment of love and the general interaction between men and women on screen. 'Several films in the early 1990s transgressed the semiotics of the averted look and the aesthetics of vision and veiling with positive results' (Naficy 2003: 151). With the reinforced pressure on the tenets of Islamic rule in Iran in recent years, including the harassment of some of its most famous and well-known male film directors, it remains to be seen how this will affect the country's film industry.

The post-revolutionary Islamic leaders' decision to reinstall the veil as a mandatory item of clothing for women is still a visual sign of the sexual repression holding back secular democracy in Iran, two decades after Persson Sarvestani made her astounding debut in international cinemas with *Prostitution Behind the Veil*. The developments in the country since the autumn of 2022 are, however, a clear sign that Iranians (both men and women) from all social strata are now in favour of women's unveiling, or at least regard the veil as a voluntary item of clothing. The societal uprising this has led to makes it impossible to frame the history and culture around the veil within a post-colonial cultural studies discourse. It has become a question of women's right to liberty and equality in conversation with the feminist movement's often-heard slogan 'Women – Life – Freedom'.

Feminist documentary theory

I suggest that the widespread success of Persson Sarvestani's political documentaries is best studied using the same notion of intersubjectivity that underpins Stefanie van de Peer's study of early Arab female directors' cinema. This notion has allowed her to focus on the authorial aim and public reception of Arab women documentarists (Van de Peer 2018). I have found this analytical element equally fruitful in my effort to communicate and discuss the inherent dissidence of Persson Sarvestani's work, which embraces a transnational view on women documentarists' work in relation to its capacity to speak directly to the female onlooker. The term 'intersubjectivity' also covers the work's critical reception, in a manner which confirms that women's issues, women's rights have no borders.

In her 2018 study, Van de Peer applies intersubjectivity to allow for the creation of a tripartite relationship between filmmaker, subject and spectator, making a distinction between 'looking' and 'seeing', where the latter 'implies an ethical reconciliation between two subjects' (Van de Peer 2018: 11). Van de Peer elaborates: 'The activity of seeing is transnationally significant: if one "sees" the other through the act of looking, one acknowledges the other's subjectivity and therefore establishes a reciprocal relationship based on proximity, allegiance, understanding and solidarity' (Van de Peer 2018: 11). The act of seeing the other, and the resultant intersubjectivity it produces, fits well with Persson Sarvestani's admission that she, for instance, 'edited out footage where the mothers hit their children' (Persson Sarvestani 2011: 258, my translation) in her first international success, *Prostitution Behind the Veil*.

> On the one hand, these instances were hard proof of the women's unwellness, and I generally do not step away from the truth. But it was too crude. I was afraid that the audience ... would not be able to offer these women the sympathy they after all deserved. (Persson Sarvestani 2011: 258–259, my translation)

On her return to Iran in 1997, Persson Sarvestani's joy at being back and visiting her family in Iran was soon contested by the consistent signs of societal decline she was met with. She noted how women's quality of life had been severely diminished as well, and these revelations made her realise the necessity of replacing all sentimental feelings with a professional, critical point of view. I thus suggest that Persson's work responds exactly to Stefanie van de Peer's argument that '[b]oth feminism and documentary are grounded in the need for a material platform for freedom of expression. Both are politically inspired forms of opposition to mainstream presumptions' (Van de Peer 2017: 6). The political opposition Persson Sarvestani reflects in her work comes in the form of contextualising documentaries verifying Iranian women's hardships before and after the Islamic revolution in 1979. These documentaries vehemently contradict mainstream presumptions about Iranian history and current society that the Iranian government currently choose to publicise.

From a discursive point of view, Persson Sarvestani's admission of the above departure from the evidence-based editing formula of the documentary observational mode reflects the journalistic impetus that governs this particular film's mix of documentary and reportage, which I will address further below.

Like a journalist then, she was fully aware during the production of *Prostitution Behind the Veil* of the fact that her film would sooner or later be subject to audience reception, and she wanted to make sure the spectators could really 'see' and have pity on Mina and Fariba in their misery. I have thus opted to forego Laura Mulvey's iconic discussion of the male gaze despite its tantamount intervention in Iranian film production before the Islamic revolution (Mulvey 1975). Mania Akbari, for example, takes full advantage of Mulvey's reading of the male gaze in fiction film in her documentary *How Dare You Have Such a Rubbish Wish*.

I have also opted to forego E. Ann Kaplan's distinction between 'looking' and 'gazing' along the lines of gender and race (Kaplan 1997), in favour of Van de Peer's very acute observation that, above all, 'seeing' the other is key when it comes to obtaining a more productive intersubjective understanding based on solidarity and sympathy between filmmaker and spectator (see Van de Peer, 2018, Introduction). My discussion of the public reception of Persson Sarvestani's work is thus based on Van de Peer's fruitful concept of intersubjectivity, allowing for both the director's own transnational status as a feminist documentarist and focused on Western-type political activism, with a clear aim of raising the onlooker's awareness of the sociopolitical situation in post-revolutionary Iran.

The combination of the underlying intersubjectivity connoting Persson Sarvestani's cinema and her films' incessant preoccupation with the fight for women's democratic rights in Iranian society allows me to compare them to documentaries produced by Western second-wave feminist directors in the 1960s and '70s on equal terms. They are motivated by the same ambition to make the spectators aware of women's vulnerable and precarious situation in society at a certain point in time. This observation brings me in turn to Julia Lesage and the final paragraphs of her essay 'The political aesthetics of the feminist documentary film' (Lesage 1990). In this essay, Lesage addresses different affinity groups, such as consciousness-raising groups, whose agency and politics were recorded by feminist documentary filmmakers in the United States for public exhibition from the late 1960s to the early 1970s. She concludes that:

> Third World Women mediamakers [*sic*] often deal explicitly with women's issues, usually tracing them out in a broad social context. They take up issues of sexual politics, especially rape, reproductive rights, and prostitution. ... They show women struggling to enter the public sphere on an equal footing with men. They frequently present an angry view of the sexual double standard. The women who speak in these films often speak with the voice of the disenfranchised and poor. Such media works speak to women viewers across national boundaries [and] it is clear that these films are structured in ways that seek to convey generalisations that we can call 'feminist'. Their wider distribution will create a more profound sense of a 'women's community' that exists throughout the world. (Lesage 1990: 344)

Re-periodising, which is to say *extending*, second-wave feminism to apply to societies outside Europe and North America that struggle under patriarchy has represented a scholarly domain since the beginning of the twenty-first century. Lesage's above conclusion from 1990 – that documentaries about the struggles of women from developing countries should be labelled as feminist – is pertinent when discussing Nahid Persson Sarvestani's first two documentaries from 2004 and 2007. Both films invite me to position them as pertaining to Western-style second-wave feminist documentaries, formally inscribed in a news documentary framework, because of their consciousness-raising topics. My discussion of Persson Sarvestani's feminist interventions in these documentaries is thus directly tied to making the world aware of the widespread poverty, drug addiction and prostitution in Iran, as well as the effects of such an obsolete institution as polygamy after the religious revolution. The abundant patriarchy has resulted in women being denied basic human rights, including gender equality and prosperity.

Why not accented cinema?

Given the above discussion of the feminist theory that underpins my analysis in this book, my earlier statement that Persson Sarvestani's documentary interventions regarding the effects of the Islamic revolution in Iran on its people allow me to generally dispense with Hamid Naficy's theory of accented cinema in all except two of her films should make sense (Naficy 2001; Ulfsdotter 2019). I shall, however, briefly revisit Naficy's notion since both *Seventeen Years of Longing* and *The Queen and I* (2010) reflect a clear ambivalence when it comes to upholding a critical, distanced point of view in relation to the films' topics, and thus show a certain adherence to Naficy's first category of accented cinema dealing with exilic denial. According to Naficy, such films are 'motivated by both the desire to disavow the ruptures of exile and the wish that it will be short-lived, culminating in a glorious return' (Naficy 2001: 77). Unlike the typical 'accented' fiction film of this type, it is my contention that Persson Sarvestani's documentaries instead reflect a indirect ambivalence that springs from the documentarists' eternal struggle to withdraw from personal engagement with the documented material in favour of a merely professional approach. In terms of epistolary content, such a fluidity emphasises and pivots on the authorial mark on the finished film product. I shall therefore be revisiting Naficy's exposé to further emulate these particular aspects of accented cinema in my discussions of Persson Sarvestani's documentary practice below. I begin by taking this early opportunity to explain why it is not possible to generally position her work within Hamid Naficy's notion of accented cinema.

When compared to Persson Sarvestani's work, her production process is, for instance, not dependent on 'the interstices of social formations and cinematic practices', nor is it 'critiquing the deterritorialized conditions of filmmakers' (Naficy 2001: 4). From an epistemological point of view, Persson Sarvestani's documentaries, as a rule, do not involve 'the use of the formal properties of letters and telephony to create and exchange meaning', nor does she challenge 'the authority of the classic realist films and their omniscient narrator and narrative system' to convey and discuss the topic at hand (Naficy 2001: 5). From a more discursive point of view, her films do not explore 'transitional and transnational places and spaces, such as borders, tunnels, seaports', nor does her mature work revolve around 'journeys of and struggles over identity' (Naficy 2001: 5). I could go on, but seen as a whole, the major reason why Nahid Persson Sarvestani's film practice does not compare with the cinematic processes and disposition of accented cinema is that this production mode primarily engages with feature-film production, whereas she is a political documentarist. She is not out to fictionalise either historical or current events.

In terms of categorisation, Hamid Naficy divides the 'accented' feature film productions made by exiled Iranians in America (his domicile, hence a natural and easily accessible study material for his book) into six different categories dealing with themes such as denial, panic, pursuit; or Iranians in transit in third spaces, or returning to Iran in search of a home (Naficy 2001: 77–78). Only one of the less pronounced themes pertaining to the category 'cinema of return' is of initial interest in connection to Nahid Persson Sarvestani's film production, and these are films made by 'documentarists who returned to document the 1979 revolution and its aftermath' (Naficy 2001: 78). This is important here because regardless of Persson Sarvestani's above-mentioned first documentary feature, *Seventeen Years of Longing*, the installation of the Islamist regime in Iran did nothing to change her critical views of Iranian society in that film. Far more interesting, and unexpected, is the flow chart covering certain unexpected formal aspects reminiscent or directly related to the tenets of accented cinema that found its way into *The Queen and I*, as already mentioned.

Generally speaking, there is an important difference between the director's work and accented cinema in that Hamid Naficy's presentation of the concept does not include any critical aspects or discussions of gendered, documentary film interventions. In her memoir, Persson Sarvestani never refers to any outright agenda equal to Western-type feminism during her youth in Iran. Instead, her political interests were rooted in traditional 1970s Marxist ideology which foregrounds a society based on gendered equality, if not democracy. It suggests that one of the reasons she entered a Marxist student group was its awareness-making efforts on the topic of social class and the economy, given the underlying patriarchal and hierarchical rule that permeated the Iranian society she grew up in. Persson Sarvestani thus recognised and embraced the camouflage of the sewing workshop she ran in her free time as an opportunity to talk with the Iranian women she met there about a free and equal society 'without the patriarchs looking over my shoulder' (Persson Sarvestani 2011: 99). On the topic of feminism itself, she mentions that while still living in Iran, she also had the opportunity to write on 'social and women's issues' of interest to her as a politically aware but still not formally trained journalist at a local paper (Persson Sarvestani 2011: 109).

Efforts have since been made to revisit and theoretically develop Naficy's idea of accented cinema in order to add a gendered and even outright feminist dimension to it. One of the first scholars to approach accented cinema in this manner was Asuman Suner (2007), claiming that productions normally categorised as belonging to a country's output of 'national cinema' because they were made by directors living inside the country's borders can, in fact, also be read as accented cinema film products (Suner 2007: 66–67). Taking her thesis a step further, she goes on to suggest that two films by a Turkish and Iranian woman director, respectively, could even be situated 'within a "transnational feminist" framework, if feminism is not conceived solely on the basis of the assumption of hegemonic Western feminism' (Suner 2007: 67). Suner's concept is thus based on post-colonial theory, and it was later picked up and further refined by Pinar Fontini (2022). Fontini also plays down the importance of physical deterritorialisation by claiming that a feminist accented director could also be characterised as one living a 'culturally exilic' life in her own country (Fontini 2022: 2). First applying and then honing Naficy's original definitions of accented cinema for her own purposes, Fontini posits that '"accented" feminism indicates a difference between the standard, regular, institutional feminism and another feminism', by which she means a feminism that is different from the 'hegemonic, pure, Western' original (Fontini 2022: 9). Elaborating further, she writes that 'accented feminism includes the national, racial and gender-related dynamics within its context and creates a multi-dimensional, diverse womanhood' (Fontini 2022: 10). Fontini hence also aligns her discussion of accented cinema within the tenets of post-colonial theory, which is a discursively big step away from the classical formalism that underpins Naficy's original characterisation of the notion.

I furthermore claim that neither form of 'accented feminism' is applicable to Persson Sarvestani's feminist documentary practice since she is based in Sweden, where she also received her professional training as a journalist and TV documentarist. Both her career and documentary practice are framed within a Western-style publishing tradition based on a free press and its affordances, as her memoir confirms. Seen as a whole, these circumstances warrant a different framework for Persson Sarvestani's documentary activism. I consequently turn to the notion of societal patriarchy as one of the basic discursive tenets of my discussion of the feminist agency that forms such a natural and integral part of Persson Sarvestani's films. My textual observations of these are based on examinations of the production processes of the films, their political and activist agency, and certain formal aspects, such as their visual construction and narrative structure.

Self-reflexivity and subjectivity in first-person documentary practice

There can be little doubt that the surge in documentary filmmaking in the essay mode since the beginning of the twenty-first century is a result of the rapid development of digital technology, above all, the mobile camera phone. Instilling phones with cameras, which can be used to both take pictures and record moving images, gave average, individual citizens the opportunity to document events taking place around them. Add to that the rapid spread of digital media and use of online communication to spread information, then the fast-maturing development of the personal camera which constitutes the essence of the essay film mode begins to make sense.

Starting out as a TV journalist in the common interest domain in the late 1990s, it follows that Persson Sarvestani began her career as a feminist documentary filmmaker specialising in Iranian subject matter with two films in the expository mode in the early 2000s (see Nichols 1991). *Prostitution Behind the Veil* and *Four Wives, One Man* were both made to feature length and reflect a production mode and editing perfectly aligned with general TV documentaries. It was rather their thematic framing and narratives related to women's issues that revealed that they were primarily intended for exhibition in cinema theatres to select audiences, as well as the international film festival circuit.

Persson Sarvestani's approach to her subject matter then changed considerably during the few years between the release of these two traditional documentaries and the following two, for two main reasons. The first reason is of course the above-mentioned technological development of filming and exhibition equipment, which completely changed the conditions for using witness documentation as epistemological 'proof' material. The new material conditions meant that the documentarist profession also had to take a new direction. The second reason is directly linked to events which had a decisive impact on Persson Sarvestani's personal life and hence affected her authorship. I will reflect on both trajectories in detail below. What is interesting from a theoretical perspective is the director's new mode of documentary address, which now veered towards the first person, framed by outspoken self-reflexivity and a subjective camera.

Through different aesthetic forms of self-inscription, such as voice-over, talking to the camera, including footage of the production process, interaction with documentary subjects and performance, this particular documentary practice is now readily known as filmmaking in the essay mode, framed by a personal, often political, voice (see e.g. Renov 2004; Lebow 2008; Rascaroli 2008, 2009; Alter and Corrigan 2017). This mode has framed all Persson Sarvestani's documentaries since 2008, which exhibit the above aesthetics in various forms. According to Laura Rascaroli, the 'presence-absence of the enunciator is a key point of the essay film', which means that Persson Sarvestani's personal view and approach to factual events especially sustains her documentary work (Rascaroli 2008: 38). The author mainly comes to the fore via the voice-over, since 'one of the key elements of the essay is the direct address of the receiver' and is as such 'a privileged tool for the author's articulation of his/her thought ... and hence a prime location of the author's subjectivity' (Rascaroli 2008: 38–39).

Beyond the physical expression of the Self, films in the essay mode also exhibit a reflective component. According to Alisa Lebow, 'there are two distinguishing features of the first-person documentary: subjectivity and relationality' (Lebow, 2008: xi). Applied to Nahid Persson Sarvestani's essay films, this duality has been expressed through a dialogue which has taken both political and emotional turns. I offer the example of *Anders, Me and His 23 Other Women* (Persson Sarvestani, 2018) as an instance in case because it is the most autobiographical of all her works. This film documents the director's endeavours to find a new partner after her divorce in the mid-2010s. Showing her daily trawling on Tinder to find a suitable man, she tells us about all the unsuccessful dates she has been on – until she started dating Anders. Turning out to be a dream man, he is easy-going, forthcoming, charming, sportif and enjoying life. They have lots of fun together, and the director is visibly very much in love with him. But he does not commit to the relationship in terms of wanting to move it forward, rejecting her invitations to live together, to spend even more time together. Having so bravely turned the camera on herself, ready to share her private life with the onlooker, it becomes almost painful to see her so lovesick and forlorn. Until, that is, she collects her wits and starts asking *why* Anders does not want to enter a more serious relationship with her. He makes no secret that he enjoys everything about her person, so how can it be that he is so evasive on this important point?

After many twists and turns, Nahid gets her hands on the notebook he always carries with him. In it, she finds the contact details of no less than 23 other women and the *extremely* elaborate schedule of his meetings with them. What is more, some of them do not live locally in the Stockholm area. The mind-blowing, not to mention emotional, shock makes her ill, and anyone less strong than her would, I think, have had to permanently break off the relationship. But Persson Sarvestani did not. After limited recuperation, she managed to contact a couple of the women he also dated and told them about the situation. She was allowed to film interviews with them where they discussed 'men' and Anders in particular. These women were clearly as gaslighted, shocked and repelled as Persson Sarvestani was. Then came the confrontation with Anders – again on camera – showing their demands that he explained not so much his conduct but how it was emotionally possible for him to conduct his life like that. It transpires that he was quite content with the set-up, happy to not make any long-term life planning, just taking the days as they come. He did not express any emotional regrets at all, and even carried on making publicity for the film with the director. It was not until after the film premiered that *his* problems began when all his girlfriends disappeared overnight. He even tried to sue the director over the film, claiming 'personal damages'.

From a critical and intellectual point of view, *Anders, Me and His 23 Other Women* is an excellent example of Persson Sarvestani's discreet but still readily manifest feminist interventions in the essay film mode. Her film exposes patriarchy's borderless and ingrained goal to control and shape women's lives to its own benefit. Alisa Lebow is therefore right when she points out relationality as one of the main features of feminist cinema in the essay mode precisely because regardless of 'the fact that we believe it to express our individuality, it nonetheless also expresses our commonality, our plurality, our interrelatedness with a group, a mass, a sociality, if not a society' (Lebow 2012: 3). By underlining the importance of this particular characteristic in the essay film's ontology, Lebow also opens up political cinema's geographical transnationality. I thus suggest that Persson Sarvestani's new approach to her documentary filmmaking process, style and subject matter in the late 2010s was primarily a result of increasing awareness of the global commonality of her main subject matter – patriarchy and women's rights. Enforced geographical restraints on her documentary practice and individual mobility also played an important role in this change in her authorial approach, as we shall see.

Authorial divestiture

Having thus presented the general theoretical tenets that underpin my discussion of Nahid Persson Sarvestani's documentary practice, it still remains to be said that the most important theoretical notion for my charting of the director's trajectory as a filmmaker is 'authorial divestiture'.

Originally coined by Cecilia Sayad, she refers to authorial divestiture in relation to Jean-Luc Godard's comment at the end of *Weekend* (Godard, 1967) where he announces 'his shift from romantic cinephilia to political militancy, soon to be followed by the transition from auteurism to collective authorship in collaboration with the Dziga Vertov Group' (Sayad 2013: 41). Sayad does not comment on what Godard's authorial 'move' actually entailed, but looking into the storyline of *See You at Mao* (Godard, 1969), for instance, the film narrative seems to unveil a traditional communist agenda:

> Filmed in the UK in 1969, this documentary by Godard and the Dziga Vertov Group represents an analysis of production and the status of women in capitalist society and a speculation about class consciousness and the need for political organisation. A group of men formed by trade unionists and employers debate on what measures would benefit their respective classes. At the same time, a group of young hippies tested several Beatles songs. (IMDB, downloaded on 18 January 2023)

Two pieces of information on the IMDB site have a bearing on my argument regarding Persson Sarvestani's transition into authorial divestiture: first, *See You at Mao* is categorised as a documentary on the site. Second, when it comes to the film's writer and director, Godard's name is accompanied by that of Jean-Henri Roger (IMDB, downloaded 18 January 2023), which is to say that two persons made the film. In Godard's next documentary made in collaboration with the Dziga Vertov Group, *Pravda* (1970), the persons credited for writing and directing the film include a third party, by the name of Paul Barron, according to the site, whereas Godard himself is not credited for any work on the film in either of the released film texts.

In her further discussion of authorial divestiture in relation to Jean-Luc Godard, Cecilia Sayad references Kaja Silverman, who claimed that Godard constantly reconfigured his practice through authorial death, based on the fact that he 'defined the author as [a mere] receptacle' (Sayad 2013: 41). Sayad confirms that 'Silverman's conceptualisation of Godard as receiver also matches the director's definition of himself as [an] antenna of the world' (Sayad 2013: 43).

Persson Sarvestani's trajectory towards a more fluid and divested form of directorship in her documentary practice does not in any way match Godard's Romanticised view on authorship. Authorial divestiture and how it connects to Persson Sarvestani's oeuvre is, however, my foremost scholarly preoccupation in this book. Instead of authorial Romanticism, I shall elaborate on the hypothesis that present-day authorship in documentary filmmaking pivots on a post-modern type of liquid authorship introduced by Zygmunt Bauman in the early 2000s (Bauman 2000). Griselda Pollock sets the scene:

> Bauman invites us to consider the relations between the shift from solid, defined, localized, territorialized, nation-bound modernity to that which he has defined as liquid rather than *post* modernity. In this qualifier, liquid, Bauman catches up the effects of globalization, migration, nomadism, tourism, the effects of world-wide webs and internets, socket-free phones and texters: a world and its transforming subjectivities redefined by inter-action with the huge and fascinating potentials of new technologies and information systems. (Pollock 2007: n.p.)

Outline of the book

This book is divided into three parts, each covering two films by the director and presented in chronological order. Each part begins with a short introduction in which I lay out the main topics of discussion in relation to both documentary and feminist film theory. I then move on to provide an introductory discussion on the films at hand, both separately and in conversation with each other.

This division seems natural to me for two main reasons. The first one is merely numerical in that the ensemble of films addressed here cover three decades and roughly saw the release of two films in each. The other reason is that a chronological presentation of Persson Sarvestani's documentaries allows me to concurrently map her professional career as a documentarist in relation to both the films' subject matter and increasing hybridity, moving towards authorial divestiture.

The first two films, *Prostitution Behind the Veil* and *Four Wives, One Man* are products of a *mixed authorial process* based on journalism and an observational mode of documentation. They reflect Persson Sarvestani's background as a TV journalist, with the latter film showing an increasing awareness of aesthetic properties.

Based on a thematic discourse, these films introduce Persson Sarvestani as a politically explicit enunciator in the expository mode, presenting 'a commentary on ... public issues that affects not only them, but also the culture and society at large' (Rascaroli 2009: 13–14). Her voice-over narration is offered in Swedish, suggesting that the films were meant to enlighten a non-Persian-speaking audience on the topic of Iranian women's precarious situation. As we can see from these films, bridging matters like heroin-addicted prostitutes and polygamy demands a lot from the filmmaker in relation to the documented individuals, the resulting documentary narrative and audience reception.

The second phase resulted in *The Queen and I* (2008) and *My Stolen Revolution* (2013), which embrace the *essayistic documentary mode* and *first-person narratives*. Again, the latter of the two films reflects a clearly discernible documentary hybridity by making way for both re-enactments and a divested form of authorship.

After being ordered not to return to Iran in 2006, Persson Sarvestani forged a new documentary strategy, launched in the 2010s, primarily based on the inscription and performance of her Self as a vital component of the film narrative. Her participation transpires either on the discursive level or in a more readily physical form in a discursive mode typical of the self-inscriptive first-person documentary (Yu 2019). From *The Queen and I* onwards, Persson Sarvestani has taken an active part in the performance of the narrative in all her political films.

Regardless of this new auteurist approach to her documentary practice, and the fact that Persson Sarvestani is an outright political filmmaker when it comes to her documentaries on Iran, I raise the question of whether *The Queen and I* fits the remits of accented cinema based on its 'comparative exilism and diasporism' (Naficy 2001: 85) despite the assumption that this notion relates primarily to fiction or art films.

My Stolen Revolution revolves around a group of exiled Iranian women's experience of being jailed for their political acts of resistance during and shortly after the Islamic revolution. The film's documentary premise (the women's on-camera testimonies of the atrocities to which they were subjected in Iran) quickly becomes explosive because Persson Sarvestani insists on her own inscription and performance in the narrative. Her insistence almost overturns the project because they all know that Persson Sarvestani never took part in the political counter-activities of the 1980s which led to these women's incarceration, nor was she even brought to trial for being politically active in Iran.

Her failure to turn *My Stolen Revolution* into a self-inscriptive first-person documentary with her at the centre heralds instead her further transition into a form of authorial divestiture, a notion to be discussed further below. When used to its full potential, the polyphony of testimonies in *My Stolen Revolution* introduces a hybrid element to the film's overall narration and complicates its narrative. Although the reason for these women's suffering can be traced to the same source, the many layers of stories bring the narrative of the single voice-over into question, and Sarvestani Persson's enunciator with it.

The last phase of Persson Sarvestani's documentary practice discussed in this book saw the release of *Be My Voice* (Persson Sarvestani, 2021) and *Son of a Mullah* (Persson Sarvestani, 2023). Both documentaries retain a divested type of authorship but announce yet another documentary approach by Persson because of their remediating character and the latter film's involvement with digital media. I base my discussion on the hypothesis that these films show the director's further involvement with Celia Sayad's idea of authorial divestiture while still adhering to many of the directorial principles framing the first-person documentary. The director's inscription and performance of her Self has become a vital component in her more recent films, as I already mentioned. In *Be My Voice*, she makes her hitherto strongest performance both at a discursive level for the spectator and as Alinejad's intellectual and physical counterpart in the film. Persson Sarvestani's increasingly pronounced presence on a discursive level is essential for my analysis and discussion of her authorship trajectory as documentary filmmaker. The films' overall narrative development indicates a general move towards authorial divestiture, which, according to Celia Sayad, reflects a conscious transition from auteurism to collective authorship. The full potential of such a documentary strategy and a more contemporary, necessarily fluid type of political activism is manifested in Nahid Persson Sarvestani's *Son of a Mullah*.

PART ONE

Prostitution and polygamy: two close-ups of patriarchy

- *Prostitution Behind the Veil* (2004)
- *Four Wives, One Man* (2007)

Introduction

Part One explores how the reiteration of evidence in the form of narrative, filmed footage and editing inform Persson Sarvestani's early documentary film practice in the expository mode. The discussion of the ontological character and terms of production of *Prostitution Behind the Veil* in particular also suggests that both the documentary mode of film production and essay cinema are suitable generic frameworks for a discussion of the transnational subject matter dominating Persson Sarvestani's work at this point.

I copied the title of this section directly from Nahid Persson Sarvestani's memoir, *Always in My Heart* (Persson Sarvestani, 2011: 255). In this part of the book, the discussion of her first two feature-length documentaries, *Prostitution Behind the Veil* and *Four Wives, One Man*, revolves around their common denominator, which is the vulnerability of certain groups of Iranian women under hegemonic patriarchy. Of the six films Persson Sarvestani has made so far, only these two were filmed inside Iran. As a result of the screenings of *Prostitution Behind the Veil* for Iranian audiences, events that occurred while she was back in Iran to shoot *Four Wives, One Man*, Persson Sarvestani was taken into custody by the Iranian authorities and interviewed at length about her business in the country. Following these interviews, she was announced persona non grata in the country and had to leave before she had finished shooting her new film. An attempt to hire a local filmmaker to record the last scenes failed and resulted in Persson Sarvestani's daughter Setareh eventually going to Iran to complete the shooting – after having had to wait for her visa for two years (see Persson Sarvestani 2011).

Two important assumptions thus inform this section. On a textual level, Persson Sarvestani's original, politically grounded interest in women's issues may well have been increased by men's general harassment of Iranian women in the country's visual culture during the 1960s and '70s. Mania Akbari's above-discussed compilation of excerpts from Iranian fiction films entitled *How Dare You Have Such a Rubbish Wish* provide many pertinent examples, regardless of the fact that some of the films were labelled as comedies. Akbari's film documents Iranian men's seemingly unrelenting sexual badgering of young women on screen during the entirety of the country's popular film history from the silent era until the 1970s. It is accompanied by the director's voice adapting Laura Mulvey's theory on the male gaze and how women were sexualised and objectified on screen in this film genre. Akbari's compilation gives us an idea of what Iranian audiences could expect from their national film industry and the visual crudeness it used to confirm ingrained traditional customs of female oppression. The 'film farsi' genre was immediately abolished by the Islamic regime after the revolution in 1979.

The excerpts of popular films in Akbari's documentary and her accompanying voice-over commentary, however, make Barbara Molony and Jennifer Nelson's discussion of a prolonged and transnational form of second-wave feminism covering an extended 'time period... to embrace the decades immediately following the Second World War and into the early twenty-first century' sound reasonable (Molony and Nelson 2017: 23). Taking this long view of second-wave feminism 'would encompass the work of activists not included in the narrow band of US and European feminism confined to the 1960s and 1970s' (Molony and Nelson 2017: 3), thus making the tenets of this feminist wave applicable to a general discussion on women's situation in Iran during the time period Persson Sarvestani's first two films were conceived in 2004–2007 as well. Akbari's documentary also allows me to discuss the political aesthetics of Persson Sarvestani's documentaries from the point of view of the narratives and cinematic presentations commonly seen in documentaries by second-wave female documentarists, as already discussed.

The second assumption regarding her first two documentaries that needs signalling is that from a production perspective, *Prostitution Behind the Veil* and *Four Women, One Man* are the only two out of the six films under discussion that were filmed in situ in Iran. Both films thus spring from Persson Sarvestani's personal meeting with and vehement reactions to the disarray and dysfunctional society that had evolved in Iran since she left the country. 'As an exiled Iranian I wanted compensation for all the years the Iranian regime had deprived me of. I was prepared to do anything I could for the Iranian people and challenging Iran's oppressors' (Persson Sarvestani 2011: 254).

Subsequently, the topics of these films were picked with political retribution in mind, and for obvious reasons rendered Persson Sarvestani the stamp of persona non grata from the Iranian authorities. She cannot and should not attempt to officially go back to Iran under the current regime.

1
Not accented cinema: *Prostitution Behind the Veil* (2004)

In *Prostitution Behind the Veil*, her first feature-length documentary for an international audience, Persson Sarvestani very quickly establishes herself as the author of the narrative through the inscription of her own persona in the footage. But even more important is her voice-over, which has a neutral, informative character. She begins by reminding the spectator of the early promises made by the Islamic state to offer the Iranian people democracy and free elections. Persson Sarvestani then counters this false promise by filming the severely impoverished and sick beggars in the streets and the loitering youngsters, until the military police suddenly turn up and ask for her papers and filming permit.

> I walked the streets of Shiraz with my film camera ... alert to anything worth documenting in the post-revolutionary Iranian society. ... The inhuman sexual repression established by the regime made women vulnerable and isolated, and supported the men who continued to suppress their own women. (Persson Sarvestani 2011: 257, my translation)

The main focus of the director's account is the social situation of Iranian women in post-revolutionary society, and she points out some of the poignant setbacks they have suffered. In short, she lets us know through the voice-over that Iranian women have been deprived of full Iranian citizenship since the revolution. Persson Sarvestani draws a parallel between her own standing as a Swedish citizen with full rights and Iranian women's rights to judicial equality, which are now only half of those available to Iranian men. Women's testimonies in court count for less than men's, women inherit only half as much of an estate compared to men, and women are at all times the subjects of their male counterparts. This radical change in women's citizenship was made possible through one effective streak of judicial abuse whereby the religious clergy proclaimed that Iranian girls were to be treated as adults at the age of nine. From this age, they are fully judicially accountable in relation to the Iranian state and eligible for marriage, housekeeping and work. Contraception has been prohibited during long periods of time. The figures relating to the number of young female fugitives on the streets of the bigger Iranian cities that Persson Sarvestani offers in the film's voice-over are obviously no longer applicable, but the problem still exists. The country's religious leadership has furthermore claimed that it does not tolerate either drug addiction or prostitution. (For more information see, for example, Wikipedia.)

Prostitution Behind the Veil tells an incredulous story about many Iranian women's atrocious living conditions in Iranian society, and the film's visuals (but not the narrative) are in many ways corroborated by the social misery reflected in *The Ladies' Room*, introduced above. When it comes to the two prostituted women portrayed in Persson Sarvestani's documentary, the director writes in her memoir that the truth was that, like many other women: 'Neither Mina nor Fariba had ever lived with men that were not violent towards them or their children. They were both prostitutes selling their bodies at a low price. They had both become addicted to heroin [through their former husbands]' (Persson Sarvestani 2011: 258, my translation).

As already mentioned, *Prostitution Behind the Veil* won the Golden Nymph Award at the Monte-Carlo Television Festival in 2005 for Best News Documentary, thus launching her international career. The award corresponds well with the contents of the director's factual voice-over and overall production mode. She confirms the characteristics of her approach in her

Figure 1.1 Fariba with her son waiting for a suitable customer, *Prostitution Behind the Veil*. Screenshot by author.

memoir, where she remarks that she had by then developed a documentary process which was journalistic in style, focusing on the individual and the matter she wanted to investigate (Persson Sarvestani 2011: 254). Given her earlier career as a documentarist for Swedish Television, and the film's categorisation at the Monte-Carlo Television Festival, I take my cue from Julianne Burton (1990) and suggest that *Prostitution Behind the Veil* is an example of the type of social documentary Burton discusses in *The Social Documentary in Latin America*. Burton's provisional definition of this type of documentary pivots on the mutual configuration of 'a human subject and a descriptive or transformative concern' (Burton 1990: 3). Further according to Burton, 'most filmmakers combine aspects of various modes in their work to achieve a particular effect, in a given cultural context, at a specific historical conjuncture' (Burton 1990: 3). Using Bill Nichols' original typology of different documentary modes as a matrix, the most rewarding modes to work with when making a social documentary are the expository, observational, interactive and reflexive modes (Burton 1990: 4–5).

Looking at the formal aspects of *Prostitution Behind the Veil*, I contend that it reflects a combination of the observational and expository modes in that it provides a stringent voice-over, images of observation predominantly in the form of long takes and a mix of sound types (both non-synchronous and synchronous sound).

> We look in on life as it is lived. Social actors engage with one another, ignoring the filmmakers. Often the characters are caught up in pressing demands or a crisis of their own. This requires their attention and draws it away from the presence of filmmakers. The scenes tend, like fiction, to reveal aspects of character and individuality. We make inferences and come to conclusions on the basis of behavior we observe or overhear. (Nichols 2010: 174)

Nichols adds the proviso that in the observational mode, '[t]he filmmaker's retirement to the position of observer calls on the viewer to take a more active role in determining the significance if what is said and done' (Nichols 2010: 174). However, Persson Sarvestani's expository voice-over is above all pivotal for a Western audience when it comes to communicating what we are actually looking at, and what it means in relation to the overall scheme of things. Burton thus emphasises that the social documentary is an instrument for cultural exploration and epistemological inquiry. As such, it provides counterinformation capable of challenging hegemonic societal structures by exhibiting 'the testimony of individuals and groups who would otherwise have no means of recording their experience' (Burton 1990: 6–7).

Mina and Fariba let Nahid Persson Sarvestani film their open-hearted and private conversations, including their demonstrations of wounds and scars that men have given them over the years. Mina testifies on camera that her current *sighe* (temporary 'husband') has severely knifed and kicked her, and Fariba's sister-in-law reveals that Fariba's former husband sold their three-month-old daughter for a couple of hundred pounds. And yet they hope to somehow ascend to better lives for themselves and their children. In reference to the intrusive and condescending documentary approach shown in the above-mentioned Iranian documentary *The Ladies' Room*, Persson Sarvestani's treatment of her documentary subjects is cautious, empathetic and polite. She interrupts her recording to take care of the children when the mothers are either out working or on a high.

Documentary strategies in *Prostitution Behind the Veil*

Expository documentary mode

From a narrative and documentary point of view, Persson Sarvestani additionally offers a male perspective through the middle-aged Habib, who originally introduced her to Mina and Fariba. They all live in a once-impressive townhouse, now occupied by all sorts of squatters, including themselves. Habib is a fortune teller who has trained his two budgies to pick up envelopes with good news from a box for the paying customer. His lawful wife has remained in their house in the countryside, while he buys the company of young women for a fixed period through an equally lawful *sighe*. The spectator learns how, when his latest young woman runs away with the money he offered her for six months company after two weeks, he offers Fariba to take over the position once she has 'cleaned up her act'. Always looking for money, Fariba gives it a try, but Habib immediately starts controlling her every movement and Fariba calls it off. In no way despondent, Habib shakes his shoulders and goes looking on the streets for another young women on the run. In summing up, the visual and reiterated behaviour of Iranian men towards women is clearly reflected by the director in the voice-over, with Persson Sarvestani declaring that contempt towards women had reached what seems to be a constitutional level in Iran by the turn of the twenty-first century.

Figure 1.2 Mina and Fariba share a large room in a squalid former townhouse, *Prostitution Behind the Veil*. Screenshot by author.

As Julianne Burton demonstrates, the social documentary practice is not new, but the many international awards for *Prostitution Behind the Veil* tell us, first, that the topic itself was unexpected. It is the first documentary about the post-revolutionary, socially precarious situation of Iranian women under Islamic rule screened for international audiences. The images are paired with Persson Sarvestani's voice-over in an open attack on the new rulers' neglect of the Iranian people, and women especially. This direct address is different from the commonly found impartial comments made by filming television journalists. The film's social and ethical impetus is also further confirmed by the fact that Persson Sarvestani went looking for Mina and Fariba when she returned to Iran ten months later. To her delight, she found Fariba in a new, more healthy relationship and rid of her addiction. Mina's destiny sadly remains unknown.

Second, the international acclaim for *Prostitution Behind the Veil* confirms that Persson Sarvestani achieved her authorial goal of presenting a documentary which pairs cold facts with empathy for the victimised and disenfranchised Iranian women – without becoming sentimental. From a feminist theoretical perspective, the overall politically charged, subjective point of view of *Prostitution Behind the Veil* introduced Persson Sarvestani as a foremost feminist documentarist in the tradition of the awareness-raising efforts of second-wave Western feminists in the 1960s and '70s. Julia Lesage has explained that 'if the Feminist [sic] filmmakers deliberately used a traditional "realist" documentary structure, it is because they saw making these films as an urgent public act' (Lesage 1978: 508). In her view, the main characteristics of 1970s feminist documentary were '[b]iography, simplicity, trust between woman filmmaker and woman subject, a linear narrative structure, little self-consciousness, about the flexibility of the cinematic medium' (Lesage 1978: 508), resulting in documentaries that are 'filmed to combat patriarchy' (Lesage 1978: 509).

Based on the filmed subjects' everyday life experiences in *Prostitution Behind the Veil*, Persson Sarvestani's film has an overtly political intent to present consciousness-raising issues related to the vulnerability of Iranian women and their subjectivity, but also to inform international screen audiences about the actual situation of some women in post-revolutionary Iran.

In tandem with Persson Sarvestani's background working for Swedish Television, the inception of and reception to *Prostitution Behind the Veil* is thus explained by its journalistic form. Still, the film's outright engagement with second-wave feminism is pronounced in a clear voice and positions it within the feminist documentary genre. According to Bill Nichols, '[the] voice distinguishes documentary films. We sense a voice addressing us from a particular perspective about some aspect of the historical world. This perspective is more personal and sometimes more impassioned than that of standards news reports' (Nichols 2010: 147), and this is what ultimately allows me to describe *Prostitution Behind the Veil* as a social documentary in line with Burton's categorisation.

From an Iranian perspective, and my effort to re-periodise second-wave feminism to frame Persson Sarvestani's early documentaries, a diachronic discrepancy seems to occur between her contemporary documentary practice, especially the directness of her voice-over narration, and the visual narrative and subject matter displayed in *Prostitution Behind the Veil*. On review, the combination of a second-wave documentary feminist approach and the film's contemporary content is explained by Iran's geographical location, society and rule.

The overall subject matter – Iranian women's suffering in a patriarchal society – has many analogies with ideological topics in consciousness-raising documentaries from the 1970s such as *Growing Up Female* (Julia Reichert and Jim Klein, USA, 1971) and *Self-Health* (Catherine Allen, Judy Irola, Allie Light, USA, 1974), even though the Western film product predominantly reflects white middle-class women's perspectives. Although documentary activism with a feminist purpose was not a household formula at the time, I argue that Persson Sarvestani's documentary approach was necessitated for practical and political reasons, since her goal was to spread the word that Iranian women still lived under unacceptable patriarchal rather than Muslim rule. It therefore seems to me that the narrative in *Prostitution Behind the Veil* first and foremost references the early feminist documentary's goal to inform and educate, in this case, foreign audiences (Lesage 1978).

Julia Lesage's study of Valeria Sarmiento's work concurs with Hamid Naficy's claim that auteurship is one of the basic tenets of accented cinema (Naficy 2001). As already mentioned, my aim with the hypothesis informing this study of Persson Sarvestani's documentary practice is to demonstrate how a unique, fluid mode of auteurist documentary film production has developed over three decades, where the apparatus and film topic have evolved in tandem with changing political developments and documentary modes for maximal audience impact. Echoing not Naficy but Lesage on Valeria Sarmiento's documentary practice, Persson Sarvestani could be described as having 'adopted a mode of production common to many independents. She prefers an artisanal, self-directed work process. She works within the tradition of the political avant-garde, in which the artist understands politically the need to create a new film/video language in order to take on new or unexplored social and personal themes'. (Lesage 1990: 326)

Like Persson Sarvestani, Sarmiento in *A Man When He Is a Man* (Sarmiento, 1982), for example, took on machismo (male privilege), but not without adding Latina women's complicity in their own oppression by accepting different cultural patterns leading to 'idealized, traditional gender roles perpetuated by the myth of romantic love' (Lesage 1990: 320).

As a pioneering scholar on the topic, Lesage thus posits two interesting observations about Sarmiento's work; first, that '[p]erhaps only the woman artist working alone or as an auteurist director can take on the most taboo themes' (Lesage 1990: 328). Second, she suggests that Sarmiento's film practice may well have been enforced by the very effects of the geographical distance between her native Latin America and exiled domicile in France: 'It is perhaps because she had to go into exile that she developed both the aesthetic skill and the syncretic overview that allowed her to create work with analytic power' (Lesage 1990: 326).

To sum up, Lesage's overall discussions of second-wave feminism and its bearings on film work by women of varying nationalities offers a fruitful point of departure for my scholarly endeavour. This approach involves embracing a dual discourse pertaining to both the political content and the evolving liquid documenting process that frame Persson Sarvestani's films about human rights, post-revolutionary Iran and its people.

2

Hegemonic patriarchy and polygamy: *Four Wives, One Man* (2007)

In her next film, Persson Sarvestani wanted to confront one of the most traditional forms of hegemonic patriarchy in Iran, after it had been reintroduced by the Islamic regime, namely polygamy. She had asked her father to help her find a family practising this marital form who were also ready to discuss its social effects on camera, accepting the fact that the resulting documentary would be seen by foreign audiences. At this point in 2004–2005, unauthorised excerpts of *Prostitution Behind the Veil* had begun to spread to Iran via the internet, and the director had encouraged Fariba and her son to leave the country for their safety. The unwelcome purpose of Persson Sarvestani's political activism, to reveal the Islamic regime's devastating impact on Iranian society, was quickly followed by relentless harassment of her on her return to the country to shoot the new film. She knew her visit would be cut short sooner or later, so she stayed with the chosen family (her documentary subject) and recorded as much as she possibly could of their daily lives. The Iranian authorities kept on increasing their pressure on her, and she was forced to leave Iran after only three weeks of filming. The project could not be finalised until two years later when her daughter Setareh managed to officially travel to Iran and continue documenting the family. On Setareh's return, Persson Sarvestani unofficially entered the country and was immediately put under surveillance. She still managed to spend a full day with Heda and his family, documenting the final scenes for the film (Persson Sarvestani 2011: 263).

The two-year delay in the film's completion is not verified in the documentary itself but is textually important as the relationship of the husband, Heda, to his wives was unintentionally allowed time to progress during the intervening time. Certain aspects of his actions thus came to a head during the second period of documentation and contribute important information to the film's overall narrative.

Taking a closer look at the film's textual level, *Four Wives, One Man* begins with an orally uncommented quote from the Quran, in which men are encouraged to take two or even three wives, if they can afford it. The film's main narrative revolves around the 50-year-old, financially successful sheep farmer Heda, his four wives and 20+ children. Heda boasts to the director that he can afford to have so many wives because he has managed to successfully rent out his combined harvester for many years. Hearing one of his friends honestly declare on camera that he is satisfied with having only one wife apparently has not changed Heda's mind. Quite the opposite, as we shall see.

Persson Sarvestani writes in her memoir that in the beginning Heda thought it was a film about him, which may explain why all four wives play up to the camera and confess how much they love and adore him at the very beginning of the film. 'We are totally dependent upon him. If he dies, we all die,' says one of the wives. 'He is the father of our children so we must love him,' says another. Heda's threat to give them a good beating if they did not do their best in front of the camera may also have had something to do with these false love tokens (Persson Sarvestani 2011: 261).

Very slowly and not before Heda himself has confessed to his unwaning sexual needs and lust for women, the film's focus steadily changes to build an argument against polygamy based on the testimonies of his four increasingly unhappy wives. The women offer their stories and opinions voluntarily as outbursts of agony or sadness in short sequences edited as if they were outspoken monologues, void of any interruption from the director/film photographer. The candidness with which they are given suggests that the women – like Heda – felt they could fully confide in Persson Sarvestani on the topic of polygamy and the emotional misery this type of marital arrangement causes the women. All four wives attest to their unhappiness about finding themselves in a polygamous family situation. This form of family composition had been none of the women's wish.

The degree of their joint unhappiness is unexpectedly – and perhaps unwittingly – confirmed by none other than Heda's own mother, who lives with his first wife, Farang. As a woman of 75 years, Heda's mother was brought up under the late Shah's rule when polygamy was not authorised. She lived in a monogamous relationship, married to Heda's father, and they had five sons together. In the documentary, she openly alleges that polygamy has a detrimental influence on the younger generations, especially the women. Persson Sarvestani's documentary makes it very clear that Iranian women's worth is nowadays negligible – at least in the most underprivileged groups in society. It is never made clear whether any one of Heda's wives can actually read or write.

The first and fourth wives are the most unhappy ones. Farang, the eldest, shares the information that she and Heda were happily married for eight years before he started courting his female cousin, Goli, and took her as his second wife. With the new housing arrangements, Farang now manages not to see Heda very often and cites heart problems as a reason why they can no longer have sex. It would seem that Heda and Farang have seven or eight children together, and one or two grandchildren when Persson Sarvestani started documenting them in 2004. In a private talk with the director, Heda intimates that Farang is still his one and only true love. His words seem to be confirmed by the other wives, who all admit to feeling more or less emotionally 'disposable', as confirmed by Heda's pronounced disinterest in his children.

Ziba is introduced as Heda's fourth wife at the beginning of the film, and she had been married to him for two years when the documentary project was initiated in 2004. She was divorced from a drug addict at the time she married Heda. Since she is the youngest of his wives, and not yet a mother, she helps Heda with the sheep farming and also does a lot of the cooking for his vast family. Still in her twenties, Ziba is already deeply and permanently marked by the fact that she does not seem able to conceive. This failure stings Heda, making him irritable, and he vows take a fifth wife – a threat which has already, by 2004, resulted in two suicide attempts by Ziba.

On the documentarist's return after a two-year suspension, Ziba has become a foster mother to the latest child of the third wife, Shahpar. In a comment, Shahpar says that she felt sorry for Ziba and decided to give her own newborn daughter as consolation. Ziba seems very happy to perform the tasks and duties of a mother, and the little girl seems to truly love her. Her relationship with Heda has not improved over the past two years though. Trailing after them in the early morning hours out on the grounds towards the end of the film, the camera witnesses Heda's outright rejection of Ziba as his wife. He mercilessly announces that he is now looking to marry a virgin who will obey his orders and satisfy him sexually without delay or apprehension. Ziba's desperate fight to stay on as one of Heda's wives, Heda's threats and his eventual fulfilment of them at the very end of *Four Wives, One Man* and its implications for Ziba's future, soon makes the spectator identify her as the film's unquestionable, exceedingly vulnerable, main protagonist.

The film's overall discourse, and especially Persson Sarvestani's effort to rightfully portray these women's unhappy fates through several talking-heads interviews, is concurrent with that of the women featured in *A Fatal Dress: Polygamy* (2009) by the Turkish filmmaker Mizgin Müjde Arslan. In her above-mentioned study, Pinar Fontini emphasises the importance of witnessing on camera to construct female agency: '[Arslan's] documentary reveals the marriage experiences of the women through their own voices, [thus] constructing their agency' (Fontini 2022: 3).

As if polygamy is not enough, Persson Sarvestani's documentary also brings up the age-old tradition of *sighe* in connection to both *Prostitution Behind the Veil* and *Four Wives, One Man*, in her memoir. Banned during the monarchic rule, the current Islamist regime encourages *sighe* as yet another form of patriarchal hegemony. To put it in plain words, the constraints framing *sighe* as a socially accepted form of marital relationship in the Middle East strikes a Westerner as a religiously sanctioned legalisation of prostitution. It allows, among other aspects, Iranian men to have a marriage-like arrangement with a woman for a pre-determined term, have intimate relations with her and then leave her without consequences once the term is up. While *sighe* is often justified using moral convenience terms, the financial arrangement it entails can be seen as an act of pandering by the young girl's parents. After the *sighe* has come to an end, the woman has very slight possibilities of finding a man who will marry her for life. Her parents have no obligations to allow her back into their home, which means that she ends up as a social outcast. Whether outright *sighe* had been involved when Heda brought his fifth wife back to the house, we shall never know, but it does not seem implausible. Persson Sarvestani's footage mainly revolves around Ziba's pronounced distress and unhappiness at this outcome.

Documentary strategies in *Four Wives, One Man*

The close-up as new recording technique

In terms of Persson Sarvestani's cinematography in *Four Wives, One Man*, I would like to draw attention to two new components in her work. The first is to do with close-ups and their effects on the intersubjectivity she is looking for in her work. She writes in her memoir that at this point in her career, 'I had become interested in the close-up as a recording mode for social documentaries' (Persson Sarvestani 2011: 261).

From the point of view of immersion, this is of course the right way to go, especially since Persson Sarvestani's documentaries on Iranian subject matter were still made for a mainly Western audience at this point. Stefanie van de Peer confirms the director's authorial approach by referencing Mary Ann Doane's suggestion that the most effective way to achieve a feeling of intersubjectivity

Figure 2.1 One wife's story in *Four Wives, One Man*. Screenshot by author.

between the filmed subject and the onlooker is through the close-up of faces (Doane 2003). Van de Peer concludes that 'the close-up communicates that which is perhaps unsayable, not permissible, and counts on the spectator's sensitive understanding and really "seeing"' (Van de Peer 2017: 21). Both scholars thus trust the spectator to look actively so as to be able to 'draw out what is implicit in the political message in the film' (Van de Peer 2017: 9). More than we commonly think, achieving an effect of transnational intersubjectivity and reciprocity between the parties builds on the successful construction of a 'tripartite relationships between filmed subject, film-maker and spectator', according to Van de Peer (2017: 9).

It is true that in *Four Wives, One Man* Persson achieves a consistent impression of intimacy using close-ups. Having Heda and his family members talk directly into the camera creates a bond between them and the onlooker, which further underlines the privacy of their statements. Importantly, Persson Sarvestani is never in the frame, nor do we hear her commenting behind the camera in this film. Each family member tells their own story in monologue form, sometimes in conversation with one another, but never with the film photographer. This arrangement has the effect that their thoughts about their marital status become all the more powerful and final, especially those aired directly to camera in close-up. Persson Sarvestani writes:

> Despite the personal relationships that evolved between me and the women, I could not force the pace of the documentary process too much. It was all about waiting for the right moment and listening in, rather than trying to put pressure on their thoughts and daily routines. (Persson Sarvestani 2011: 262, my translation)

Once they were ready to confide in her, the women's intimations formally comply with the intimacy of the framed close-up. This feeling of being visually closed off at the time of the most intimate reflections on their life situations coincides with the fact that each wife had her own house and courtyard. The wives thus achieved complete privacy by being spatially closed off from one another during the act of filming, which was probably helpful given the film's sensitive topic.

Emblematic images

My second observation of Persson Sarvestani's cinematography in *Four Wives, One Man* has to do with her own ambition to fruitfully endorse moments that offer a form of emblematic visual aesthetics. 'The reason it took me so long to advance my aesthetic sensibility is because I identify so strongly with the act of documenting' (Persson Sarvestani 2011: 265).

The cinematography in *Four Wives, One Man* oscillates between being beautifully minimalistic and vividly picturesque. The director frames the candid monologues on camera in a very matter-of-fact 'talking-head' style. They were mainly shot outside, in each wife's own courtyard, using only natural light. On the contrary, the images from the family outing in an old, decrepit and completely rusty bus have an air of Fellini-esque absurdity about them that the camera completely caught as well. The muted

Figure 2.2 Family picnic in *Four Wives, One Man*. Screenshot by author.

footage from the very early morning routines when Ziba and Hera let the sheep out in the fields, covered in an early morning haze, is again very serene, and these are my personal favourite scenes. They remind me of the beautiful but harrowing chiaroscuro effect that characterises the eerie, late evening images of Fariba with her son standing by the roadside that sets the tone in *Prostitution Behind the Veil*.

Conclusion to Part One

The above-mentioned moments in *Four Wives, One Man*, however, do not detract from the fact that both films exhibit a formal matrix based on a mix of journalism and documentary styles. In terms of documentary strategies, it would seem that Persson Sarvestani is working according to the traditional tenets of journalistic exposé and Nichols' expository mode in these films, resulting in coherent narratives where the filmed footage, *sujet* and voice-over continuously echo one another. There are no textual or discursive gaps that can lead to misunderstandings in terms of audience reception. Any uncommented footage, such as when Fariba stands waiting for a punter with her son in the night, still makes immediate sense to the spectator.

The critical and scholarly reception of these films generally confirms Persson Sarvestani's auteurial purposes. *Prostitution Behind the Veil* winning the Best News Documentary award in the 2005 News Documentaries section of the Monte-Carlo TV Festival is only one example of the many awards and award nominations for this film. As a critic in *The Sydney Morning Herald* wrote:

> The footage, which includes scenes of the women soliciting on the streets and getting high in their squalid bedsits within arm's reach of their children, is harrowing. However, Persson's portrayal is sympathetic and we learn both women had led comfortable lives ruined, in part, by their husbands. (*The Sydney Morning Herald*, 19 April 2005, *sic*)

Four Wives, One Man, co-produced by New York-based Women Make Movies, was given an Honorable Mention at the Society for Visual Anthropology Film Festival in 2009. In her scholarly review Najwa Adra makes two important claims. The first concerns the polygamous tradition per se: 'The film's message appears to be the universal problem among polygynous households – a man who marries a second wife tends to lose interest in his wife' (Adra 2009: 104). The second: 'The film's major problem as a contribution to visual anthropology discourse and teaching tool is its lack of contextual information' (Adra 2009: 104). This is exactly the case. Neither of Persson Sarvestani's two films in this section are *ethnographic* films about Iran and its traditions. This means that it is of minor importance that we do not know exactly where in Iran they were shot, or the ethnographic history of the women's work as carpetmakers in *Four Wives, One Man*, their household chores and how their houses are spatially set up. For instance, it takes a good while before we learn that Heda's three older wives in fact make a living as carpet weavers at all. Instead, Persson Sarvestani made these films as an effort to inform international audiences about the effects of hegemonic patriarchy and social disenfranchisement on the lives of especially vulnerable women in Iran. Based on the visual impact of the close-up, these are consciousness-raising films looking to establish an intersubjective bond between the Iranian women and international female audiences to improve their precarious situation.

In his above-mentioned film review introducing five documentaries by female filmmakers of Iranian descent, Reza Poudeh's positive acclaim on their usefulness as introductory films about different aspects of mainly Iranian culture is generally the same for all five productions. His remarks on Persson Sarvestani's *Four Wives, One Man*, however, reveals that he is aware of the film's underlying criticism of polygamy. He writes:

> Although documentaries (and narrative films) produced in Iran after the revolution have focused on social problems in the country, Iranian filmmakers living outside the country who are unconcerned about government censorship, have been more daring in the coverage of social issues which implicate the Iranian government. (Poudeh 2010: 413)

Poudeh does not make any similar claims in relation to any of the other four films in the review. I thus suggest that his opinion is based on Persson Sarvestani's immodest choice of translation of the verse from the Quran which introduces the film's topic: 'Her choice of translation places the documentary in the context of a Quranic verse that states that taking four wives is religiously sanctioned as long as the husband can 'provide' for all four wives, all other considerations aside' (Poudeh 2010: 413). This is completely true, of course, and Poudeh consequently puts forward the caveat that he is not entirely sure if Heda can actually 'marry the fifth wife according to Iranian/Islamic law' (Poudeh 2010: 414). Should this be the case, it would mean that *Four Wives, One Man*, like the director's previous documentary, reveals the Iranian patriarchy's additional opportunity to victimise women through the temporary marriage arrangement *sighe*, likewise encouraged by the Iranian government.

Authorial agency

Outright or not, both *Prostitution Behind the Veil* and *Four Wives, One Man* come through as *counter-narratives* compared to the other films discussed by Poudeh in his review. My conclusion is confirmed by the fact that Nahid Persson Sarvestani has been persona non grata in Iran since excerpts, and sometimes the complete version, of *Prostitution Behind the Veil* reached the Iranian public in 2005.

In *Women's Cinema, World Cinema: Projecting Contemporary Feminisms* (2015), Patricia White claims that 'their authenticity as women born in the countries with which their work deals are delivered with the class and cosmopolitan credentials of women of culture' (White 2015: 89). In addition to being highly cultivated, the typical cultural capital of exiled Iranian artists and feminists is characterised by education, liberal values, fluent English and moving in Western art circles (White 2015: 89). Most of the characteristics she thus attaches to this female dissident persona rightly have a bearing on well-known Iranian diasporan women directors of fiction and art-house film, but not documentarists dedicated to investigative journalism – and certainly not Persson Sarvestani. She arrived in Sweden in her early twenties and had yet to formally train for her profession as a journalist. She took additional courses in film direction as part of her labour market education programme to become employable. White's assertion, that '[t]hese directors' worldwide reputations as Iranian exilic artists and feminists position their debut films as part of their dissident personae', is, however, a fitting categorisation of Persson Sarvestani's first two films (White 2015: 89). It should be noted, however, that White subsequently frames exilic Iranian art-house cinema by female filmmakers mainly within Hamid Naficy's notion of accented cinema in her book. Teamed with her original interest in women's issues as a teenager still living in Iran, it hardly comes as a surprise that Persson Sarvestani, in both her films documenting women's situation *inside* Iran, voices none of the art-house directors' cultural capital but consistently speaks with the dissident's political voice. The two documentaries discussed in this section thus represent poignant feminist counter-narratives based on investigative journalism. The director's critical approach sets the tone for her entire documentary oeuvre on the topic of women's situation in Iran during and after the Islamic revolution in 1979, despite the fact that she can no longer film *inside* the country. Persson Sarvestani's evolving practice of female authorship is nevertheless an outright expression of feminist activism very much unlike the successful diasporan women directors outlined by White, but not without a certain affinity to Naficy's documentary category of 'cinema of return' mentioned above (Naficy 2001: 78). With her first two films, Persson Sarvestani positions herself as a clearly dissident persona, dedicated to producing consciousness raising, matter-of-fact counter-narratives based on re-periodised second-wave feminism. Looking ahead, her future film narratives confirm my suggestion that they compare better with the type of counter-narrative benefitting the female point of view introduced by Claire Johnston in the early 1970s than Naficy's production mode of 'cinema of return' (Johnston 1973).

Having explored the effects of an expository mode mixing journalism with documentary practices in *Prostitution Behind the Veil* and *Four Wives, One Man*, Part Two of this book introduces Persson's decision to draw on self-inscription as a technique of the Self in her ensuing films.

PART TWO

New narrative and formal interventions

- *The Queen and I* (2008)
- *My Stolen Revolution* (2013)

Introduction

As a result of the international screening of the *Prostitution Behind the Veil* and *Four Wives, One Man*, Persson Sarvestani became persona non grata for life in Iran in the mid-2000s. I posit that this physical and geographical limitation also forced an unexpected professional shift in her documentary practice. In short, it led to Persson Sarvestani applying the grand narrative of Iran to her own history and first-person filmmaking, encouraging *expanded* journeys of personal, factual and intellectual discovery as a way forward in her professional career. This authorial process consisted of self-inscription in tandem with a new form of expanded authorship in her next two films, *The Queen and I* and *My Stolen Revolution*.

While she was indeed banned from entering Iran and therefore could not continue making documentaries reflecting Iranian women's current living conditions in situ, the ensuing transition into first-person documentaries was also propelled by personal loss. She was still grieving her young brother Rostam's death, and in deep need of finding closure by way of information about his time in prison and last days of life. Both factors spurred her transition into a more self-reflective mode of documentary filmmaking.

Looking back, both films engage with her family situation against the background of Iran's grand narrative. *My Stolen Revolution* is also very much the director's answer to the enforced spatial restraint she now must heed. This polyvocal documentary asserts the precarious situation of Iranian women through a new type of visible evidence, in a new documentary mode.

Auteur cinema can be described as a type of signature filmmaking and is primarily found within fictional genres. In these cases, the director turns the film script into a personal product bearing their hallmark of consistency in style, content and cinematography. Certain modes of documentary filmmaking make similar allowances for subjectivity and self-inscription, as demonstrated in contemporary interactive and expository documentaries like Malik Bendjelloul's *Searching for Sugar Man* (Sweden, 2012) and Michael Moore's *Michael Moore in Trumpland* (USA, 2016). The inscription and performance of the Self is a vital component in these works, regardless of whether it is performed merely on a discursive level or manifests itself as more readily physical (see Nichols 1991; Bruzzi 2000; Rascaroli 2009; Yu 2019).

From *The Queen and I*, a pattern of self-inscription emerges and becomes a key component in Nahid Persson Sarvestani's work, which means that I do not consider her early television documentary *My Mother, A Persian Princess* to embrace the tenets of this form of performative subjectivity. When she now opts to conduct her documentary practice in accordance with a pronounced auteurist documentary mode, it is still performed in relation to discursive remits that are open-ended, feminist and political.

The strong manifestation of a first-person camera at work in both *The Queen and I* and *My Stolen Revolution* thus signals the end of Persson Sarvestani's practice of the traditional expository documentary mode. Applying a mode of self-inscription allows her to fuse her personal history with the grand narrative of Iran's post-revolutionary history in these two essay films, in response to the following claim by Michael Renov:

> The Montaignean essay derives in part from disparate precursor forms – the confessional or autobiography as well as the chronicle ... Descriptive and reflexive modalities are coupled; the representation of the historical real is consciously filtered through the flux of subjectivity. (Renov 2004: 70)

The Queen and I and *My Stolen Revolution* confirm the diametrically opposite 'realities' that make essay film an open documentary film format rather than a firm genre. This openness to both experimentation and individuality in fact favours the development of the director's unique authorial practice. Her films thus clearly indicate that '[essay film] is the expression of a personal, critical reflection on a problem or set of problems' (Rascaroli 2008: 35). Citing Paul Arthur, Rascaroli (ibid.) reiterates that 'a quality shared by all film essays is the inscription of a blatant, self-searching authorial presence', which brings her to the role of the enunciator:

> This authorial voice approaches the subject matter not in order to present a factual report (the field of traditional documentary), but to offer an in-depth, personal and thought-provoking reflection. At the level of rhetorical structures, in order to convey such reflection [*sic*], the cinematic essayist creates an enunciator who is very close to the real, extra-textual author; the distance between the two is slight, as the enunciator quite declaredly represents the author's views, and is his/her spokesperson. ... The essay's enunciator may remain a voice-over or also physically appear in the text, and usually does not conceal that he/she is the film's director. The narrator of the essay film voices personal opinions that can be related directly to the extra-textual author. (Rascaroli, ibid.)

The consequence of such a close proximity between the author's and enunciator's rhetorical standing in relation to the textual commitment allows the enunciator to address the spectator 'directly and attempts to establish a dialogue. The "I" of the essay film always clearly and strongly implicates a "you" – and this is a key aspect of the deep structures of the form. [The] "You" is called upon to participate and share the enunciator's reflections' (Rascaroli, ibid). This 'You', then, is always the embodied spectator, encouraged to engage with and reflect on the subject matter presented by the enunciator. This rhetorical assumption echoes Van de Peer's above discussion of 'intersubjectivity', the notion she applies to allow for the creation of a tripartite relationship between filmmaker, subject and spectator.

In the hands of Persson Sarvestani, the essay film's indirectly activist, repeated interventions are meant to dismantle the grand narrative she presents in her documentaries, which consequently makes the pact with the spectator an essential requisite. Rascaroli suggests that it is 'this subjective move, this speaking in the first person that mobilizes the subjectivity of the spectator. ... [asking] the author's personal reflection to be either shared or rejected by the viewer' (Rascaroli 2008: 36–37). In terms of its rhetorical structure, the direct address to the spectator via voice-over is a key tool, making it 'a prime location of the author's subjectivity; as well as the main channel of the enunciator's address to the spectator' (Rascaroli 2008: 39).

This pact reflects the essay film's initial raison d'être and consequently has much in common with both the expository documentary mode and second-wave feminism in that all three discourses aim at enlightenment, or consciousness-raising if you like. It provides a starting point for my discussion of Persson Sarvestani's subjective filmmaking and its bond with documentary formats neighbouring essay film, given some of its distinctive features:

1. Essay films have 'a well-defined, extra-textual authorial figure as their point of origin and of constant reference';
2. 'they strongly articulate a subjective, personal point of view';
3. 'they set up a particular communicative structure, largely based ... on the address to the spectator, or interpellation' (Rascaroli 2009: 3).

According to Rascaroli, the film's interpellation is performed through an outright gesture directed at the viewers. 'The subjective enunciators of first-person films often address spectators directly, sometimes by looking into the camera lens, or else by speaking to them [in voice-over], or simply by presenting their discourse as a confession, as a shared reflection, or as a persuasive argument' (Rascaroli 2009: 14). By underlining the *dialogical* quality of the essay film proper, Persson Sarvestani's transition into essay film mode gave her full access to 'a stronger impression of authorial presence' compared to the expository documentaries she had produced earlier (Rascaroli 2009: 14). Cecilia Sayad has established that this particular documentary format also engenders an intertextual authorial presence through the emphasis on the director's corporeal presence and self-inscription in the film frame. Such performances of authorship involve the director becoming 'an "actor" instigating behaviours through questions or the proposition of artificial (or semi-artificial) situations' (Sayad 2013: 75).

More importantly, both scholars apply the pronouns 'they' and 'their' as a further indication of the director-auteur-enunciator's post-modernly fractured Selves and different ways of imposing their authorship on a particular work. I mention this now because, as already intimated, the post-modern idea of the individual as existing in continuous flux is a key component of my thesis for this study of Nahid Persson Sarvestani's documentary practice. However, I hold that in relation to her work, the 'fractured Selves' Rascaroli and Sayad mention evolve into a yet more diverse form of divested authorship, whereas the role of the enunciator remains intact.

To sum up, in this introduction I posit that by embarking on a new documentary journey related to Iranian matters around 2010, the subjective framing and the director's persistent authorial presence in *The Queen and I* and *My Stolen Revolution* are features that indicate a break with the expository mode and journalistic exposé of her two previous documentaries. In terms of audience success, I cannot say if her new mode of documentary filmmaking is at all connected to the fact that these two films have had less success in the film festival circuit. *The Queen and I* was nominated for the Grand Jury Prize of World Cinema – Documentary at the Sundance Film Festival in 2009 and received Swedish television's Kristallen Award for Best Documentary in 2010. It was also awarded the Prix Italia in 2009. *My Stolen Revolution* fared somewhat better with two nominations and two honourable mentions (Los Angeles Film Festival, The International Association of Women in Radio & Television's festival in Casablanca, Morocco, and Abu Dhabi Film Festival), and in 2016 received the Award of Excellence for Socially Relevant Film at the Winter Film Awards in New York.

I have already discussed Persson Sarvestani's approach to authorship in the essay film mode in these new films (Ulfsdotter 2019). To move the discussion forward, revisiting them for the purposes of this book presents a welcome opportunity to explore the films' cinematic fabrics along slightly different avenues of investigation. In this part of the book, in addition to keeping the auteurial tenets of essay filmmaking in mind, I introduce a new reading of *The Queen and I* through the lens of Hamid Naficy's well-known notion of accented cinema. I then proceed to expand on Sayad's pivotal notion of authorial divestiture to further pinpoint the development of Persson Sarvestani's documentary activism in *My Stolen Revolution*. I ask myself: in what manner do these two documentaries respond to and advance such characteristics typical of essay filmmaking as 'informal, sceptical, diverse, disjunctive, paradoxical, contradictory, heretical, open, free and formless' (Rascaroli 2008: 39)?

3

Auteurism in accented cinema mode: *The Queen and I* (2008)

My scholarly discussion of Nahid Persson Sarvestani's documentary *The Queen and I* is partly based on the following quotations from her memoir:

> It was impossible for me to stop making critical films about Iran, especially after the humiliation I was made to suffer when the authorities detained me in 2006. The unpleasant Iranian police officers accused me of being a monarchist – when I had in fact agitated for the Shah to leave to country – which gave me the idea for my next film, focusing on the Shah's wife Farah Pahlavi who has survived as a symbol for a highly superior but genuinely hated regime.
> (Persson Sarvestani 2011: 291–292, my translation)

> I could not forego her grief over Khomeini coming to power, obviously, since I shared it with her. But I did find her relativisation of the events offensive when she proclaimed that it was the revolution that had destroyed our lives. I knew, after all, that it was the leftist movement [and our call for democracy] that had fuelled it. And yet I could not deny the fact that a certain comradeship emerged between Farah and me across that vast divide when it came to the new regime that had now expelled us. (Persson Sarvestani 2011: 293, my translation)

> It may well be that I was too accommodating in my relation to Farah. But I at least allowed myself to be forthcoming, to tread new ground, and pose trying questions. Having

> forged a close, personal relationship with her also made it more difficult for me to approach her from a merely political point of view. (Persson Sarvestani 2011: 296, my translation)

The intellectual, political and creative implications that can be unpicked from the above quotations from Nahid Persson Sarvestani's memoir are key to my renewed discussion of *The Queen and I*. To begin with, they offer a clue as to why the director chose the structural openness of the essay film as her new documentary format. As for its contents, the spectators are 'asked to take the film as its author's subjective reflection and to connect with her, to share or reject her line of reasoning' (Rascaroli 2009: 14). This appeal also embraces Persson Sarvestani's transition into a new type of textual voice, the self-inscriptive first-person documentary.

Laura Rascaroli's introduction of essay cinema's interpellative nature, in this case its heretical interventions, also explains why and how Persson Sarvestani's auteur uses Iran's grand narratives for her own personal and critical purposes (Rascaroli 2009). One of its main points is using self-inscription as a method to confirm and justify her subjective point of view and, ultimately, the film's narrative. The most striking example in her catalogue is *The Queen and I*, the director's first effort to come to terms with the murder of her younger brother Rostam, who was arrested and then executed by the Islamist regime six months later, shortly after the revolution in 1979. Her private grief over his sad fate and the trauma it caused her family initially urged the director to vindicate his death by confronting none other than the former Iranian queen Farah Pahlavi herself about it.

The non-linear trajectory of the film's unfolding, however, indicates that although the film is framed within a journey format, which, according to Stella Bruzzi, is 'structured around [chronologically disclosed] encounters and meetings', it is of pivotal importance that the spectator understands that its enunciator could not possibly foretell 'where [the narrative of *The Queen and I* would] end up' (Bruzzi 2000: 99). In this case, the finished film tells a completely different story compared to the original *fabula* (reconciliation topic) envisioned by the director. Persson Sarvestani's effort to place her authorial vision (artistic idea) centre stage is in fact already thwarted at an early stage. The director's inability to even introduce it to the film's fabric leads to her enunciator being inadvertently disturbed, as is the investigative and progressive quality of the traditional reiteration of the journey format she had anticipated.

Again citing Stella Bruzzi, 'the presence of the author is a significant *intervention*' (Bruzzi 2000: 99, my italics) in this narrative format, but in the case of *The Queen and I*, the director's intended journey never came full circle by providing closure. Instead, it left her where she first started. The main reason for this failed interpellation is that Persson Sarvestani's meetings with the Queen never really focused on her brother's death, which means that, from a formal point of view, the use of self-inscription for that particular purpose was not fruitful. Still, positioning *The Queen and I* as an instance of subjective cinema based on an intellectual journey of factual discovery and self-reflexion, we shall see that the performative agency of Persson Sarvestani's Self became a highly *unpredictable* component of the film, something of a loose gun. In this case, it resulted in the enunciator and self-inscribed director becoming friends with the original political enemy, utterly foregoing her initial authorial vision.

Regardless of whether this Self occurs in physical and visible form, or merely in voice-over, it has a decisive impact on the film's narrative and form in terms of visible evidence, not least vis-à-vis the spectator. The question is therefore how this reflects on the agency of the female auteur having lost direction, with the film taking on a completely different textual voice.

Beside Persson Sarvestani's performative intervention, an important feature in *The Queen and I* is the organic manner in which the highly ambiguous narrative is reiterated through her candid unveiling of the 'weaving of the process of thought into the text' via her own voice-over (Rascaroli 2009: 193, n. 11). The journey format, with all its unexpected turns, is made particularly clear by the open-ended dialogues between the director and Farah Pahlavi, since these were not scripted beforehand or otherwise prepared. The resulting liquid transparency of the film fabric undoubtedly makes the film both personal and dialogical, perfectly in tune with filmmaking in the essay mode. Persson Sarvestani's extra-textual authorial figure thus allows the film's fabula to take on a more pronounced *liquid form*, indicating the way in which the director embraces the fact that she simply cannot anticipate what will be said during their conversations. I here introduce liquid form as a discursive tool derived from Zygmunt Bauman's ideas on liquid modernity as an individual, chaotic, ambivalent and uncertain notion; in short, lacking a communal, permanent and reassuring structure just like the essay film mode itself (see Bauman 2000).

Persson Sarvestani's continued physical appearance in the film is theoretically linked to Bill Nichols' participatory documentary mode, used in fluid combination with Rascaroli's declaration that although the presence–absence of the enunciator is key to essay film, the direct address to the onlooker is equally essential for reasons of clarity (Rascaroli 2009: 37). This discursive requisite is put into practice when Persson Sarvestani shares the ordeal she goes through, when Farah Pahlavi unexpectedly calls off her participation in the film project, with the onlooker. The audience next sees how the filmmaker manages to persuade the former queen to resume their collaboration by unveiling the real reason why she wants to make the film, or almost. The strong dialogical relationship Persson Sarvestani has by then established between the film's enunciator and the onlooker comes into full play in these sequences (Rascaroli 2009: 35) because the onlooker is as perplexed as the filmmaker herself when faced with this unexpected obstacle. In fact, Farah Pahlavi delivers this threat not only once but twice during the film's production. Both the director and onlooker immediately realise that Pahlavi's final decision could put an end to the entire film project, but thanks to the strong relationship that had developed between the director and Pahlavi when the second hiatus occurred, the fear of having to abandon the project was quickly resolved through a candid exchange of personal thoughts and political opinions.

I suggest that Persson Sarvestani's decision to include these difficult and hazardous passages in the finished film fabric has a dual purpose; it is first of all a truthful reiteration of the journey format as a partly unpredictable working process. Second, by contrasting these unexpected turns of events with her private thoughts expressed in the film's voice-over, the enunciator puts the essay film's strong self-reflexive character into full play.

Finally, by extending and dramatising the film's fabula, the director simultaneously defines the hybrid and outright ambiguous quality characteristic of the essay film. In summing up, Persson Sarvestani's original micro-narrative (discussing pre-revolutionary politics with Farah Pahlavi, and how her own leftist activities led to her young brother's death) was overruled by the necessity to adjust her artistic vision to Farah Pahlavi's majestic, official persona, disregarding the Romantic auteur's omnipotent presence and absolute power over her film project.

By thus letting the grand narrative of historical Iran take precedence over the film's initial topic, Persson Sarvestani's authorial influence over the film's fabula – its cinematic discourse – is thus seriously hampered and decimated. A further look at the film's textual voice indicates that the problem with its cinematic discourse lays in the discrepancy between that contributed by the voice-over vis-à-vis the displayed visuals of the comradeship between the director and former queen. All in all, this poses a serious drawback when it comes to the film's overall contribution of documentary evidence.

On closer examination, in her voice-over Persson Sarvestani laments rather than agrees that the demise of its original topic also pulls the film's narrative away from the enunciator's control. She complains rather than confirms that her growing personal involvement with the former queen has made her ideologically blind to what it really means to hobnob with deeply royalist exiled Iranians. She confesses to customising the film's content in accordance with Farah Pahlavi's wishes, to the extent that the latter was allowed to include a disclaimer regarding some of its cinematic discourse, which appears just before the end credits. The adjustment of the director's artistic vision voiced through her divergent off-screen narration is obviously a reflection of the liquid quality of Persson Sarvestani's authorial determination to do her job as an investigative documentary filmmaker.

Based on the essay film's inherent characteristic of asking the onlooker 'to take the film as its author's subjective reflection and to connect with her, to share or reject her line of reasoning', she takes the audience on this journey (Rascaroli 2009: 14). The pivotal moment occurs when she openly confesses to the audience that her reluctance to challenge the former queen over her brother's unnecessary death is due to a loss of momentum. The reason for this oversight is that Persson Sarvestani has realised that both she and Farah Pahlavi after all share the same loss (of beloved family members, of their homeland) and now also share the same destiny (a life in exile). This statement opens up an intellectual void between the film's political discourse in the voice-over and its visual narrative, which is again further enhanced by Persson Sarvestani's performing Self. The film's overall cinematic fabric remains seriously hampered by the director's ambiguous self-inscription throughout.

Having established that *The Queen and I* is formally a documentary film in the essay mode, I shall now engage with the hypothesis that some of its visuals respond to the type of 'comparative exilism and diasporism' that Hamid Naficy points out as typical of accented cinema (Naficy 2001). I have previously discarded Naficy's notion of accented cinema in connection with Persson Sarvestani's general documentary filmmaking because it mainly concerns itself with feature or experimental cinema. In view of the director's current filmography of documentaries on Iranian subject matter, and the very challenging topic of *The Queen and I*, I realise the extent to which its cinematic fabric deviates from her other productions. Consequently, my aim is to tease out the actual reason for the filmmaker's unconvincing authorial voice in this film by setting it against the aesthetic remits of accented cinema.

According to Hamid Naficy, the average accented film reflects either a state of exilism *or* diasporism. He continues: 'Exilic cinema is dominated by its focus on there and then in the homeland, diasporic cinema by its vertical relationship to the homeland and by its lateral relationship to the diaspora communities and experiences... (Naficy 2009: 15)'.

As we shall see, the overall cinematic discourse framing *The Queen and I* shows a relationship to both categories. On the topic of visuals, Naficy identifies visual fetishes of the homeland and the past as the primary markers of an accented film's visual style. These can be the 'landscape, monuments, photographs, souvenirs, letters' (Naficy 2009: 24). I suggest that *The Queen and I* in fact goes one better by revolving around one of Iran's most iconic accented protagonists: Farah Pahlavi herself. The obvious and unavoidable drawback – which I would like to think was unbeknown to Persson Sarvestani at the onset of filming – is that by selecting Iran's former queen as her film topic, the film was given an especially warm welcome in royalist Iranian circles – found mainly in the United States. The fundamental importance of Pahlavi's continuous high standing among Iranians outside their country is confirmed in their very first encounter in the film when she answers Persson Sarvestani's question about how she wishes to be addressed with the response 'Her Majesty'. As the film narrative unfolds, the onlooker comes to understand that what Farah Pahlavi really meant by that is that she may live in exile, but even so, she is an exiled Iranian *queen*. Which is to say, she sees Nahid Persson Sarvestani as a Swedish Iranian film director making an official, contemporary film portrait of her life for the exiled Iranian community.

It is therefore important to factor in that regardless of the Queen's assumption regarding the film's future audience, *The Queen and I* still features a voice-over in the Swedish language. The director thus frames the film's didactic discourse along the same lines as in her previous documentaries, to enlighten primarily Swedish onlookers. As for the film director herself, we never hear Persson Sarvestani address the Queen according to royal protocol, but she still opts for the plural 'you', equivalent to 'vous' in French.

Having positioned Farah Pahlavi as a royal, the two women are under the obligation to immediately move on to discuss the limitations of filming. The Queen makes it clear that she does not wish to be portrayed in private but only in her official capacity. In practical terms, this means that Persson Sarvestani brings the film crew along to official gatherings in which Farah Pahlavi appears in her capacity as Queen, but not to fashion shows with her close friends. The documentary footage continuously confirms this suggestion, as we see Farah Pahlavi performing duties at several official services, in various countries, including the Memorial Day of the Shah's demise at his grave in Kairo, as well as that of their youngest child at a cemetery in Paris. When Pahlavi appears in a canary yellow evening jacket at an official dinner at the Iranian royalist club in Paris, she sartorially confirms her view, and that of her entourage, on her societal position. These few seconds of documentary footage may not affect the average onlooker, but for those who know that only the Shah and his family have been seen wearing a particular shade of yellow during Iran's monarchic history, its symbolic value makes it the strongest possible exilic fetish. There is also footage of Farah Pahlavi answering letters from Iranian citizens both within and outside Iran. Even Persson Sarvestani herself becomes subject to the Queen's royal views when Pahlavi comments that the director's family should have written to her about their difficult living conditions in the 1960s. All these events explain Pahlavi's view of herself as an exiled queen acting gracefully in relation to her subjects during the diaspora.

Studying the footage covering *tête-à-tête* moments between the two women, the exilic quality of the visual content includes their joint pleasure over a small plant and its black soil brought directly from Iran as a present for the Queen. Shopping at an Iranian deli in the United States represents another piece of material, a very powerful exilic fetish. Picnicking under a parasol on the lawn outside the Queen's American mansion is yet another moment of nostalgic reverie.

Figure 3.1 *The Queen and I*. Screenshot by author.

Interspersed with their outings, Farah Pahlavi talks about her life, both before and after she became Queen, accompanied by yet further emblematic visuals, this time in the form of archival television footage. She also mentions the Shah's unsuccessful effort to calm the Iranian people's protests against his regime by promising them democratic reforms in a TV speech shortly before the Islamic revolution, and how its eruption led to the family going into exile in 1980. These histories of the destiny of Iran's royal family in relation to the country's grand narrative are repeatedly countered by voice-over statements relating to Persson Sarvestani's own family history and her escape from Iran, visually corroborated by both archival and private documentary footage and images.

This dual character of the film's overall cinematic discourse is best summed up as an example of two women positioned at the very ends of the same social hierarchy. At one end there is the Queen's official persona, reflecting a conciliatory existence revolving around her exilic being. This is conveyed through the visuals in the film, accompanied by her oral witness statements before the camera. These segments are intertwined with the selected archival visual evidence, mainly focusing on historical moments of her life during the Shah era. On the other hand, there is the director's own counter-narrative and witnessing before the camera which revolves around her becoming a diasporic subject in her own right. On the face of it, the two women's competing histories make possible a categorisation of Persson Sarvestani's film as both diasporic and exilic (Naficy 2009: 15).

However, the bottom line is that the realisation of *The Queen and I* depended entirely on Farah Pahlavi embracing the project and conceding her official persona to it. Since the film mainly revolves around her being and memory-making, its cinematic discourse necessarily becomes conciliatory overall. An unexpected confirmation of this dominating characteristic is the director's own sartorial adjustment to the visual demands laid on a person in the Queen's entourage. Persson Sarvestani returns to Paris with a completely different look when the film production is resumed after the first hiatus. Until the Queen had broken it off, the director had worn her practical, nondescript working clothes, consisting mainly of jeans and sweaters. When the two women resume their contact, the director appears on camera in formal daywear, consisting of skirts and blouses, elegant leather boots, a purse and a trench-coat. The makeover is unmistakable and can only be explained by the director's wish to comply.

I furthermore suggest that one of the pivotal narrative components in *The Queen and I* is that from a discursive point of view, the very fact that these two women from completely different social strata in their homeland met, discussed and bonded could only have taken place in exile. For this exact reason, the dominating characteristic of the visual aesthetic in *The Queen and I* morphs into creating a suitably conciliatory mood board, after having initially been set on unpacking a more interpellative, and perhaps confrontational, atmosphere.

Documentary strategies in *The Queen and I*

Addressing accented cinema

The film's visual politics thus function as a backdrop against which both the director and Farah Pahlavi appear as being exilic and friendly. This aesthetic makes it possible to categorise *The Queen and I* as a documentary pivoting on different nuances of 'denial', 'physically located in exile, mentally situated at home, and largely disavowing the fact of exile' (Naficy 2001: 77).

However, while *The Queen and I* is formally a documentary, it still does not immediately respond to Naficy's documentary category, which characterises 'accented' documentaries as 'films of return', focusing on the filmmakers' own return to Iran to try and make a home there (Naficy 2001: 77–78). Both Farah Pahlavi and Persson Sarvestani's Selves avoid all remarks in that direction, which is why I discuss *The Queen and I* as primarily a documentary in essay film format. As such, it formally displays a certain hybrid character in that Persson Sarvestani for the first time uses archival TV footage from Iranian broadcasts of the Shah and Farah Pahlavi's lives as King and Queen to provide the historical background for the film's narrative, interspersed with the women's long conversations.

I also want to share some thoughts in relation to the film's different counter-narratives, its contestatory side, to speak with Hamid Naficy (2009: 15). One, at times contestatory, side to the film consists of the more stringent, political discussions between the Queen and Persson Sarvestani, filmed during walks along the Seine or sitting in the garden of the Queen's American estate. In edited form, they are interspersed with archival footage and images. These sensitive talks also touch on topics pertaining to Iran, but relating to a more recent timeframe. For example, while they completely agree that the current situation in Iran is untenable (2007), the Queen and her entourage openly express a wish for her son to be its regent, if a new and modern 'Iran' should ever emerge. Similarly, on the topic of Iranian women's rights,

Farah Pahlavi reiterates that a woman should first and foremost be considered on the merits of professional performance rather than social modesty. Thus, I note that compared to the documentary excerpts of the Queen's official statements regarding the situation of Iranian women in the 1960s and '70's, she has obviously retained her views. This suggests that Pahlavi's position on the matter indeed was and still is on par with transnational forms of second-wave feminism discussed earlier.

This unsettling counter-narrative in *The Queen and I*, however, formally taps into both the discursive and physical inscription of Persson Sarvestani's Self in the film, in contrast to the general requirements of the Self's performance in first-person documentaries. I have already commented on the director's change of sartorial identity which strongly hampers the film's authorial voice. Still more damaging is the oral narrative presented in the unsuccessfully persuasive voice-over, in which Persson Sarvestani not only admits to losing her authorial integrity. She also admits to downplaying her own history as a political activist, and hence her own agency as both activist and professional filmmaker, to secure continued 'professional access' to the Queen. Such confessions could undoubtedly push any film project in completely unforeseen directions, but it is especially saddening here as *The Queen and I* was the director's first first-person essay film and consequently her new mode of articulation. Still, its commitment to a generic aesthetic of hybridity and narrative flexibility provided an opportunity for Persson Sarvestani to remain within the narrative framework of documentary filmmaking but also to go back over her own history. In line with my earlier discussion of Laura Rascaroli's introduction of essay cinema's interpellative aspects, this special function per se fully explains why and how Persson Sarvestani's auteur bravely customises Iran's grand narrative for her own personal and critical purposes. The director then uses self-inscription as a method to confirm her subjective point of view (Rascaroli 2009). In this case, Persson Sarvestani's candid 'weaving of the process of thought into the text', however, undoubtedly muddles its overall cinematic discourse (Rascaroli 2009: 193, n. 11). Her encounter with the former queen does indeed bestow a liquid transparency on the film fabric which makes the film more personal than her previous productions, as well as more dialogical and thus perfectly coherent with filmmaking in the essay mode. However, the discursive discrepancy between voice-over narrative and visual evidence in *The Queen and I* nonetheless results in an unreliable and liquid form of *enunciation*, which reflects badly on the agency of the female auteur and greatly harms the subjectivity at the heart of the film's narrative.

Expanding the boundaries for self-inscriptive first-person documentary

Focusing on the essay film mode itself; we must ask whether *The Queen and I* is formally as much a (self) portrait film as it is a portrait of Farah Pahlavi. The royal presented to us in the film is indeed someone whose post-revolutionary life can be defined as moulded in accordance with the general tenets of the Iranian diaspora, as is that of Persson Sarvestani herself. From this point of view *only*, they share a certain human experience as 'equals', and this suggestion theoretically frames *The Queen and I* as a double portrait of Self. Laura Rascaroli, citing Raymond Bellour, confirms this epistemological possibility when she writes on the issue of the self-portrait film that its 'coherence lies in a system of remembrances, afterthoughts, superimpositions, correspondences' (Rascaroli 2009: 171). Adding to my observations of the characteristics typical of accented cinema seen in some scenes in the film, this seems to again confirm Bellour's view on the self-portrait in relation to both the Queen and the filmmaker, in that the latter continuously inscribes them both in the picture frame.

Making a double-portrait film with Farah Pahlavi, however, meant that Persson Sarvestani had to succumb to the Queen's direction of events in accordance with the royal's different official duties, resulting in a film fabric marked by directorial allowances for discontinuity, anachronistic juxtaposition and montage. Agreeing to a narrative based on representation instead of politics, *The Queen and I* is robbed of its interpellative momentum in response to the film's original *objectif*. However, in the prologue of *The Queen and I*, by twinning the televised broadcast of the luxury and splendour of the wedding between the Shah and Farah Pahlavi in 1960s Iran with her own childhood in relative poverty, the director bridges Iran's grand narrative with the tenets of first-person documentary representation.

This is the main scholarly point of interest in the documentary about Farah Pahlavi, and the DVD release of the film includes some extraordinary extra material pointing in that direction. The footage of Farah Pahlavi arriving in an official car at the director's house outside Stockholm to meet her (Persson Sarvestani's) parents is of course utterly remarkable and proves the extent to which the Queen still thinks of herself as being under the obligations of an official role. There can be no question, though, that this event severely reduces Persson Sarvestani's professional credibility as a political activist and feminist documentarist, not to mention her claimed position as a dissident in her youth. Rightfully so, the latter claim will come be severely tested in her next film project.

Certain aspects of the aesthetics of this film, as well as some in *My Stolen Revolution*, are new and different from those in Persson Sarvestani's previous documentaries. I suggest they have an important general impact on the films' narrative discourses, and they will therefore be addressed in the conclusion of Part 2.

4

First signs of collective authorship: *My Stolen Revolution* (2013)

The following quotations from Nahid Persson Sarvestani's memoir refer to the documentary we now know as *My Stolen Revolution* as 'Prisoners of Hell', its working title:

> My friend asked me: 'Have you ever thought of making a film about all those imprisoned during the Islamist regime?' I started looking for old friends who had been subject to violence in Iranian prisons since the Islamic revolution.
>
> The 'Queen issue' however hounds me ... when I wanted to shoot a few sequences of the female ex-prisoners in Gothenburg ... they threw me out. 'You are a traitor', one of them said ... I was not allowed to film the meeting at all, and even had to leave the room. (Persson Sarvestani 2011: 297–298, my translation)

In *My Stolen Revolution*, the director brings together a group of politically involved women who had not seen each another since they were imprisoned together in Iran in the 1980s. Unlike her previous, in many ways intimate, tête-à-tête documentary, *The Queen and I*, this film emerges as a form of witness film revolving around five women who testify before the camera about their time in the same women's section for political prisoners in an Iranian prison during the 1980s. A couple of them were incarcerated for almost ten years before they managed to flee. All of them now live in different, unspecified countries and their full identities are never disclosed to the spectator.

As Persson Sarvestani's most formally complex work, *My Stolen Revolution* again offers new dimensions to her first-person, subjective documentary practice. Hence, my formal discussion of this film begins with its enunciation, authorship and narrative in relation to the formal tenets of filmmaking in the essay mode. Regarding its filmic fabric, I would like to highlight Persson Sarvestani's use of emblematic images and re-enactment to strengthen its political and aesthetic values and offer narrative relief. These points of discussion will lead to conclusions about the film's relationship to documentary witness films as well as the director's unexpected dissolution of the habitual self-inscriptive mode in first-person documentaries.

My Stolen Revolution begins with a dedication to all political prisoners in Iran written in English, followed by archival footage from Iran before and after the revolution. This archival footage is interspersed with photos of the director herself and her family from her childhood and adolescence in the country. The director's unapologetic manner of mixing images of Iran's grand narrative with her own family history works as a visual introduction, transporting the onlooker to another part of the world and setting the historical backdrop against which *My Stolen Revolution* plays out. These images are immediately accompanied by the enunciator's voice-over in Swedish, in which the narrator declares that the ideological topic of the film is to bear witness to the Iranian regime's terror and torture of political rivals at the time. On a personal level, the enunciator proclaims that with this film, the director is making a renewed effort to try and establish what happened to Rostam Sarvestani during his six-month imprisonment before he was executed shortly after the Islamist regime came to power in 1979.

After setting the historical and political scene, the onlooker sees Persson Sarvestani conducting research for the production at her desk at home. She has located her former 'boss' from the sewing studio in pre-revolutionary Iran and made contact with her. Receiving an invitation, the director goes to visit her in the United States. They have a nice time going over the memories of their work for the political group they belonged to, and the social assistance they provided by making baby clothes for disenfranchised families in their city. Persson Sarvestani assumes that they still share the same political values and goals until she witnesses the woman's devout, veiled practice of Muslim prayer in the early morning hours the following day. Her former boss explains that she had left communism for Islam to save her life, even before she left Iran. Shocked and disappointed, Persson Sarvestani returns to Sweden and begins a new search for former female political prisoners who were prepared to talk about their experiences. She found that many of them were dead or untraceable, but in the end she managed to bring together a group of five women for her film project.

My Stolen Revolution then becomes a quickly paced witness film with a shocking narrative. Only the atmosphere of emotional generosity and understanding between the women/film subjects makes it bearable to watch. Edited in short segments, it is formally a seamless two-part documentary. In the first segment the director meets each woman privately in their home and video records her witness statement about her experiences in an Iranian prison. Each witness statement is shot and framed in a relaxed but still classical talking-head set-up, and they are edited in sequence, forming the film's first segment. The finished film does not display any traces of unwillingness or hesitation to testify before the camera during these individual interviews. The procedure causes tearful pain for some interviewees though, but at least two of the women give their testimonies with a smile. Explaining the smiles, I learn from the youngest of them that because she was so young at the time she was brought to prison almost three decades earlier, time has allowed her to heal.

After having concluded these first meetings and secured the women's testimonies on film (albeit devoid of any personal details such as their full names as is customary in expository documentaries), Persson Sarvestani arranged for the women to meet for a joint discussion of their experiences during a long weekend somewhere in Sweden. As a precaution, the onlooker does not see any footage of the director preparing for this get-together, nor where it took place. The spectator only sees footage of a darkening, wintry landscape shot through the windows of the participants' unknown lodgings.

In terms of discourse and editing, the film narrative's first section consequently offers the separate witness statements, whereas the second section displays the women's group talks in condensed form. The joint scenes are shot in a similarly direct and uncomplicated manner based on the classical talking-heads mode. Both segments were then seamlessly edited in chronological order in the finished film.

It is not the polyvocal fabula of *My Stolen Revolution* that makes it narratively problematic but rather the director's insistence on self-inscription, even though she does not share the women's experiences of incarceration and torture. Already during the film's production, the director's ambition to include herself in the group caused upset among and between the women. This was perhaps not first and foremost because Persson Sarvestani never spent any time in an Iranian prison for her political activity, but rather because of her ready submission to Farah Pahlavi in *The Queen and I*. By making the previous documentary, and so to speak colluding with the enemy, she had betrayed their joint political cause of political resistance in pre-revolutionary Iran, they claimed.

These heated discussions are not included in the finished film, and I know of them only from the passage in Sarvestani Persson's memoir, cited above. However, it seems reasonable to suggest that the women's mention of disloyalty included both the director's choice of subject matter (a representative of the monarchy they wanted to abolish) and the 'accented' tropes of its visual presentation, which I discussed above. Whether or not it was the result of the disagreements between the director and the women about the current film's narrative, I notice that at least one of the women in *My Stolen Revolution* appears less frequently on camera than the others. The tormented accounts from two of them during the round-table discussions also indicate that these women may have recovered less well from their time in jail.

Still, in order to make their shared experiences of Iranian prison more tangible, some of the women offer various forms of visible, sometimes even physical, evidence. The first material item is – completely unexpectedly – the compulsory black chador and white blindfold that one of the women brought with her from prison. This 'prison uniform' was forced upon the women at the time of their imprisonment, and unexpectedly seeing it again in connection with the film production causes visible apprehension, shock and disbelief among the assembled women.

They explain that the black chador was used by the regime to make them rebound to Islam and Islamic values of female modesty, and it was compulsory to wear it outside the prison cell. They were also forced to wear a blindfold which covered their eyes, effectively cutting off their visual scope, leaving only the floor to look at. Consequently, the women were simultaneously both effectively prevented from seeing one another and unable to make out the surroundings to get their physical and mental bearings. The combination of chador and blindfold to them thus represents a form of mental torture in sartorial form. I shall return to these clothing items later, as they become a central component of the film's visual counter-narrative.

Another important piece of physical evidence that is central to our comprehension of the narrative is a clay miniature of the prison cell packed to the roof with squatting female figures. It was crafted in the West by one of the women appearing in the film to illustrate the women's living conditions in prison. Each cell measured around $18m^2$ and housed some 120 female prisoners of varying ages. Beside jointly upholding their morale, they ate, slept and washed themselves and their clothes according to a strict rota to manage the situation. Many of them had infected wounds from torture, which carried a risk of infecting other cellmates. The accuracy of the ceramic sculpture is confirmed by drawings showing similar content put on display for the camera, with yet another drawing illustrating the interior of one of the prison's torture rooms. I notice how technically well executed these pieces of evidence are, sharing none of the grit and harshness typical of clandestine photography shot in situ or sketches executed during imprisonment. More revealing or otherwise pertinent documentary images from inside these prisons do not seem to be easily obtainable for the general public.

Despite the women's efforts to jointly embrace each other's testimonies, the testimony content and demonstration of physical evidence, along with their painful effects, result in tears. Unlike the director's private interviews with the women, seeing one another again allows their memories to resurface and gain new momentum. Their reunion thus seems to also take on a therapeutic character through cooking and socialising, alongside the women testifying about their hardship on camera.

Quite unexpectedly, the physical and oral evidence they present moves the director to tears in the latter part of the film, but the women cannot really understand why. The spectator is probably not equally astonished as the film's enunciator has made it clear that in this film, the director is seeking to make amends for having inadvertently caused Rostam Sarvestani's incarceration and premature death. Persson Sarvestani explains her tears by saying that she is convinced that the military police were looking for her rather than for her brother, but ended up arresting him since she was not at home at the time of their unannounced search of the family's premises. Becoming invested in shedding light on the cruelties committed by the Islamist regime in documentary form should thus be seen as an act of atonement on her part. One or two of the women offer empathetic support, and thanks to one of the women's connections, the director finally manages to meet one of her brother's fellow prisoners. Her private quest for closure thus fulfilled, *My Stolen Revolution* also marks the directorial end of a group of essay films focusing on Persson Sarvestani's family's micro-narrative in relation to Iran's grand narrative.

Documentary strategies in *My Stolen Revolution*

Witness segments

The film contains two different types of witness segment, those recorded during private one-to-one sessions and those shot during the women's joint conversations. They are all filmed in the same type of expository mode without any audible, interrupting questions from the director. The private interviews are emotional and touch upon personal, deeply traumatic events during the women's incarceration, whereas the group discussions are characterised by a more rational and elaborate will to engage with, compare and thoroughly discuss their experiences as female political prisoners in Iran. One consequence of the latter is that once the women meet up, they seem to almost ignore the camera (and film director) during their conversations with one another. This impression is perhaps partly explained by their upset at the director's previous film about Farah Pahlavi, and their ensuing lack of trust in her. Another explanation could be that Persson Sarvestani does not in any way share their experiences of being a political prisoner. It consequently seems reasonable to assume that, when the time came to complete the film, the women had considerable control over their edited witness statements as well, if not the general editing process and final narrative per se.

Authorial divestiture

The women's attitudes to their witness depositions are thus central to the finished film narrative on more than one level, which offers an opportunity to discuss and expand Cecilia Sayad's notion of 'authorial divestiture' (Sayad 2013: 40–41). In my view, such an expanded reading of the term reflects the director's conscious transition from traditional (single-handed) documentary auteurism to a collective form of authorship, replacing the auteur's signature on the film narrative with a more impersonal, liquid quality stamp.

Withdrawing from the traditional definition of directorial authorship also occurred to Persson Sarvestani, who explained the inception of *My Stolen Revolution* with the comment that she felt an increasing responsibility to act as the voice of the people of Iran in her documentary practice (Persson Sarvestani 2011: 297). Her filmography indeed confirms this vocation, but for reasons that are anything but Romantic, either in terms of

Romantic revolutionary ideals or propelling Romantic ideas of the creative genius, like Godard's. Instead, my updated reading of authorial divestiture in relation to *My Stolen Revolution* marks the beginning of a different, more outright political activism on Persson Sarvestani's part.

To begin with, the collective form of authorship displayed in *My Stolen Revolution* may well have been a necessary directorial strategy given the women's political apprehension towards her. On the other hand, Persson Sarvestani knew full well that she was not the primary source of information with regard to the film's discursive narrative. Her film was meant to tell the women's story as former political prisoners, which meant that they had a certain impact on its *sujet*. While fully acknowledging the hybrid quality this fact instils on the enunciator, I posit that this type of shared, polyvocal authorship still has the capacity of resulting in a fully *unified* and pertinent narrative, ultimately crafted by the enunciator. The personal and joint witness statements in *My Stolen Revolution* unquestionably form a united *fabula* pertaining to the situation of female political prisoners in post-revolutionary Iran. In scholarly terms, Cecilia Sayad posits that, in relation to authorial divestiture,

> [its] performative [aspect] is partly defined by the exposure of the process. Through the performance of authorship, the studied director might move towards divestiture, shielding their subjectivities, but they at the same time figure in their film, [thus] using not so much the expression of interiority as their physical presence to assert themselves as authors. (Sayad 2013: 70)

According to Rascaroli, in 'essayistic cinema, the subject of the enunciation literally inhabits the film, and embodies in a narrator who identifies with the extra-textual author. This is what I refer to as a 'strong enuciator' [*sic*] (Rascaroli 2009: 193, n10). I thus suggest that integrating Rascaroli's idea of the 'strong enunciator' with Cecilia Sayad's ideas on authorial divestiture reflect the interviewees' standing as equally significant auteurist entities as that of the director in Persson Sarvestani's work.

The cinema interval

According to Trinh T. Minh-ha, cinema intervals 'constitute interruptions and irruptions in a uniform series of surface; they designate a temporal hiatus, an intermission, a distance, a pause, a lapse, or a gap between different states' (Trinh 1999: xii–xiii). In the Chinese language, she continues, 'the calligraphy for the word Jian, which means interval, space, partition, shows a doorway with the picture of the moon in the middle. ... The image of the moon in the doorway serenely summons up the opening of a passageway ... what enters, exits', all the while emphasising the importance of avoiding 'wolf intervals' (Trinh 1999: xiii–xiv). I posit that this type of cinema interval has an important bearing on the overall cinematic fabric of Persson Sarvestani's documentaries, especially on Iranian subject matter.

The uncommented footage in Persson Sarvestani's early documentaries discussed in the previous section was, however, still fully connected to the films' overall narratives. Those documentaries were clearly expository and journalistic, tasking the enunciator to provide general emphasis on information and rational clarity. Any uncommented images were used to further illustrate the film's single narrative and documentary *sujet*.

Self-reflexive footage offering narrative pause

New types of uncommented documentary footage offering narrative pause have since appeared repeatedly in Persson Sarvestani's practice. Pausing the textual agency of the central political *sujet* is now an especially recurring feature in her documentaries on Iranian subject matter. This footage allows the spectator a few moments to gather their thoughts around what is played out on screen. From an audience point of view, I can also confirm that offering this narrative pause has become a welcome component in Persson Sarvestani's practice because of the increasingly complicated filmic fabric pertaining to her political activism. When the director returned to making auteurist documentaries with Iranian content around 2010, the nature of this additional type of footage had changed in the same direction and may thus also consist of 'behind the scenes' footage of herself working on the documentary production. In her discussion of *Profession: Documentarist* (Sepideh Abtahi, Shirin Barghnavard and Mina Keshavarz, 2014), Lidia Merás characterises the film as 'a multi-layered documentary constructed around the uncertainties of pursuing an artistic career, while at the same time reflecting on war, political repression and nostalgia. In the best tradition of Iranian cinema, the film is also self-reflexive, foregrounding the nature and boundaries of filmmaking' (Merás 2018: 172). Merás' identification of the media format and its enunciator neatly rounds up Persson Sarvestani's approach as well since the interstitial footage she offers provides an idea about the overall production process, her studio, her collaborators, as well as her travelling to and from the recording sites. The footage as such represents additional visible evidence of not only an individual film's progression but also the construction of its narrative. It therefore cannot be argued that these scenes have always been inserted for merely ethical purposes, since she seems to always be honest about her working material in relation to different counterparts. For example, Persson Sarvestani was keen to show Farah Pahlavi the edited footage of the beginning of *The Queen and I* to regain the Queen's confidence and permission to continue shooting the documentary. Whatever the reason for its insertion may be, this type of footage propels the spectator back to the director's everyday work life, which represents a sort of neutral ground in relation to the political narrative playing out on centre stage.

It could even be argued that this footage represents a rift in the filmic fabric because it has no immediate political textual agency. On the other hand, if Persson Sarvestani had included footage from the three unsuccessful trips she made to Paris in the hope that the Queen would see her and mend the breach of trust that twice occurred and hampered the shooting of *The Queen and I*, its lack of additional epistemological relevance would most probably have led to spectator frustration, instead of offering further clarification on their collaboration.

By disseminating her political beliefs, memories and interest in – above all – women's matters across her oeuvre, the filmmaker prompts us to read her documentaries on Iranian subject matter as a diverse yet unified canvas, whose contours ultimately highlight the powerful self-reflexive nature of her auteurist approach. By applying such a perspective, I suggest that the most important and recurring type of interval in Persson Sarvestani's work is composed of short series of images and situations focusing on herself, whereby she confirms that she is indeed the film's enunciator.

Another variety of this auteurist interval occurs in, for instance, *My Stolen Revolution* and shows the director standing by the waterfront outside her house in deep thought, seemingly mulling over the right way forward. These images thus in and by themselves offer what Trinh refers to as 'an intermission ... or a gap between different states' (Trinh 1999: xii–xiii). In this case, the 'different states' would be that of the offered documentary discourse and the enunciator's legwork to produce its narrative – all done to avoid 'wolf intervals' that risk leading the onlooker to draw false conclusions from the material.

The straightforward composition of the shots of the pondering director come across as an example of a well-known subject matter in art history by reflecting an image of a thinking person of importance, such as the one we see in Auguste Rodin's sculpture *The Thinker* (France, circa 1880). This visual trope has recurred frequently in modern media, both fictional and non-fictional, most often framing powerful politicians or intellectuals. These images thus both reaffirm Persson Sarvestani's auteurist approach towards an increasingly transparent film fabric and the implications of authorial divestiture – while at the same time confirming that she is indeed the films' only enunciator. Similarly, there can be no doubt that her documentaries are the product of an overt first-person author. She is present in the films simultaneously as enunciator, narrator and as a character – and all these figures undoubtedly identify with her Self (Rascaroli 2009: 41).

Emblematic images

I next offer the term *emblematic image* to characterise another form of cinema interval in Persson Sarvestani's films. Unlike the auteurist perspective offered by the previous type of interval, this one is non-intellectual and image bound. According to Wikipedia, an emblem is an abstract or representational pictorial image that represents a concept, or an allegory, or a person, like a monarch. The emblematic image says more than a thousand words because we have an ingrained pre-understanding regarding its meaning and content. An olive branch, as a symbol of peace, is a well-known example. Its iconographic discourse separates it from the iconic image, which is typically a unique composition that has gained ubiquity through frequent publication.

I hold that the term emblematic image is a fruitful concept in relation to the cinema intervals offering representations that are intimately related to the overall textual agency of the film's narrative in which they appear without being directly addressed by Persson Sarvestani's enunciator. The reasons for not addressing them vary but sometimes seem to come across as acts of caution. During her career as a political documentarist, the director has often inserted this type of narrative pause imagery in both performative and still-life form.

Inserting an emblematic image equal to a portrait-like film still to enhance the documentary discourse in play recurs in some of the director's documentaries, after first appearing in *Prostitution Behind the Veil*. According to her memoir, it was not until she filmed *Four Wives, One Man* that she realised that '[t]he reason it took me so long to advance my aesthetic sensibility is because I identify so strongly with the act of documenting' (Persson Sarvestani 2011: 265, my translation). In my view, however, the authorial initiative to insert this type of imagery became more frequent once the director had transitioned into making documentaries in the essay film mode, and most especially in *The Queen and I*. In this film, the emblematic character of these shots infuses the narrative with a yet more pronounced 'accented' character of nostalgia by having the film's narrative revolve around Iran's former queen as the most prominent pinnacle of all 'visual fetishes of homeland and the past' (Naficy 2009: 24). Paraphrasing Lidia Merás, I suggest that these shots offer a 'nostalgic tour of the pre-Revolutionary years through [staged emblematic images], depicted here as an escape from the rigorous lifestyle enforced by the mullahs' (Merás 2018: 178). By further romanticising the meeting between a monarch and her underling by setting them up as egalitarian – well aware that it is a meeting that never could have taken place in pre-revolutionary Iran, only in a dreamed, future 'Iran', Persson Sarvestani allows the 'visual markers of difference and belonging' to add an 'accented' dimension to her narrative (Naficy 2009: 24). In this case, the above-mentioned shots of the pensive director reflect the opposite of the 'accented' stills in *The Queen and I* by projecting intellectual stamina and auteurial agency.

As with *Four Wives, One Man*, I also offer the term emblematic to describe an image's role as a visual shorthand for commonly understood cultural discourses, by resembling traditional still-life motifs. The underlying subject matter varies but shares a common characteristic in being intellectually undemanding and meant to please rather than raise opinion. Hence, these images offer stillness and a pause from the documented, real-life events dominating the film's narrative. Consequently, they often do not share an immediate connection to the film's *sujet* but always with its *fabula*.

Pantomimes

Another, more complicated form of what first looks like an 'intermezzo' or cinema interval is offered by the interviewees' enacted pantomimes appearing in the latter half of *My Stolen Revolution*. It is important to notice that these pantomimes form an integral part of the film's fabric and are presented without any form of preamble. They do, however, visually break the continuum of the ongoing discourse by being so obviously staged for the camera. For this reason, the onlooker needs some time for reflection before realising that these pantos are reminiscent of civic actions and therefore make an important contribution to the film's overall *sujet*, if not to its immediate *fabula*. Such hidden politics demand 'authorial self-consciousness, an authorial subjectivity and awareness' aligned with the essayistic mode in which Persson Sarvestani now performs her role as the film's enunciator (LaRocca 2023: 119). A well-known trope of avant-garde and experimental cinemas, the pantos themselves are visually unique to Persson Sarvestani's entire oeuvre.

From a conceptual point of view, they constitute what are generally known as expressions of *mise-en-abîme*, or films within the film, meant to further reflect the scope of the film's content by positioning it in a wider, meta-cinematic context. According to Daniel Yacavone, these 'stories within stories' either pertain '*visually* to images, screens, and frames contained within the film's image' or '*narratively*, to [the film's] nested sequences and stories' (Yacavone 2023: 90, my italics). In this case, the convoluted pantos in *My Stolen Revolution conceptually* connect simultaneously to the film's overall narrative through indirect visual reference to a certain sartorial object displayed in a previous film sequence. By *discursively* encouraging future action by alluding to past experiences, Persson Sarvestani's film within the film is set up in a very intricate manner. Christian Metz refers to this type of film within the film as *impersonal* enunciation, since the pantos in Persson Sarvestani's film do not primarily reflect back on her as the film's enunciator (Metz 1995). Instead, they clearly represent a section of the filmic text, albeit perhaps unexpected in its formulation, which is meant to represent 'a one-way stream of communication from the film work to spectator' (Yacavone 2023: 99). In this case it means that from a meta-filmic point of view, the pantos in *My Stolen Revolution* have enough enunciative power in themselves that they can both appear as part of Persson Sarvestani's documentary and communicate a message to the spectator on their own (Metz 1995: 146). Seeing as the forward-looking film-in-the-film scenes rarely occur in documentary cinema, I thus suggest that their inclusion in Persson Sarvestani's film points to her awareness of the importance of digital technology for the distribution of her work to a wider audience. I also hold that these particular spectators were already at the time (2013) accustomed to both the meaning of political memes and their reverberating importance to online activism, reflecting the younger generation's general media literacy.

The film-within-the-film sequences thus rupture the main narrative fabric both temporally and spatially while still being expressly relevant to it in terms of subject matter. In *My Stolen Revolution*, all the pantomimes are performed against the same white background, with the women recorded in semi-close-up, dressed in the aforementioned black chador and blindfold they were forced to wear in prison. Some begin by looking steadily and defiantly into the camera; others are more openly distressed, until they suddenly discard their veils and robes in either fury or pain. All women let their hair loose by shaking their heads, visually

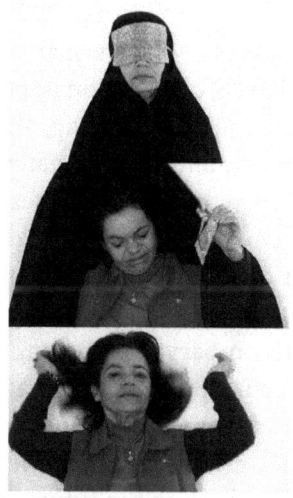

Figure 4.1 Pantomime in *My Stolen Revolution*. Screenshots by author.

embracing it and stressing its ability to move freely after having been covered and hidden away. These repeated pantomimes come across as ritualistic in character, through which they gain the ability to impress a certain message upon the onlooker.

Interestingly, the identical performances of these pantos mean that they represent a unique trope within the film's fabric, and as such both reflect back on each other conceptually and narratively per se and contribute to the film's overall content. Their reflexivity thus becomes multilayered and has, I hold, a place within a new typology of reflexive forms put forward by Daniel Yacavone. Aiming for a mid-level classification between 'conventional reflexive devices, on the one hand, and highly general functional modes on the other' (Yacavone 2023: 104), Yacavone takes his cue from Antonioni's problematisation of human perception in relation to objective truth and reality in his 1963 film *Blow-Up*. Yacavone's analysis unpacks five different iterations of inherent reflexivity in the Italian film, one of which is categorised as 'various acts of self-aware performance and role-play on the part of the protagonists' (Yacavone 2023: 104ff). Although he bases his theory on a fictional film, his further conclusion that this type of film within the film 'draws special attention to diegetic and nondiegetic roles' in my view makes his typology applicable to documentary cinema as well (Yacavone 2023: 107).

Trinh T. Minh-ha sums up the visual effect of the repeated pantomimes by stating that 'repetition is used to punctuate and ritualize a speech, thereby optimizing, through the building of rhythmic patterns around pivotal statements, its ability to empower while raising the consciousness of a community' (Trinh 1999: 45). Minh-ha's comment directly connects to two components in the pantomimes by constituting a 'pivotal statement' meant to empower the onlooking audience. As visual tropes in Persson Sarvestani's film, these performances therefore do not constitute traditional re-enactments as we know them in documentary cinema because they are not meant to reflect a historical experience. Instead, these particular pantomimes look to the future and are immediately comprehended as representing a silent, embodied intervention with a clear political message.

Dispersed over the film's latter half, the footage also reveals some of the women's initial doubts as to whether they could really go through with the performance, but also in terms of its symbolic content. Consequently, these cinema intervals are fully in line with Persson Sarvestani's feminist enunciator's vision by directly referring to the interpellation at the heart of *My Stolen Revolution*.

Zooming out, the director's intention to explore repetition and pantomime as a political trope is confirmed by Trinh's conjecture:

> I think the women's movement in the seventies [... is] for example, a movement that truly opened up a space in which politics is no longer simply to be located in these all-to-visible sites [sites and sources of official power, *author's clarification*]. It infiltrates every aspect of our lives; so that, ... instead of remaining isolated within the family context or within the individual space, these activities reflect our social function – the way we situate ourselves vis-à-vis our society, as well as vis-à-vis the world around us. (Trinh 1999: 45)

These pantomimes consequently play a significant role within the film's overall narrative structure or *sujet* despite being symbolic in character. It is, to my knowledge, the first time Persson Sarvestani uses this trope as an expression of liquid political activism. Appearing in 2013 as a joint example of silent protest, these pantomimes may also constitute the first non-verbal political call on Iranian women to reject the veil.

Conclusion to Part Two

Seen as defining documentaries of the 2010s, the textual structures in terms of focused subjectivity and address formally confirm that *The Queen and I* and *My Stolen Revolution* embody Nahid Persson Sarvestani's auteurial transition from journalistic reportage to making documentaries in the essay film mode. And yet her films do not necessarily respond to all the requisites of the essay film, in that they evince a certain hybridity in relation to its formal set-up, as well as the enunciator's agency. The evident discrepancy between voice-over and screen narrative in both films is one of the most interesting formal deviations, not least in view of the completely different documentary narrative they offer. They simultaneously reflect the director's search for personal clarification and closure in relation to her younger brother Rostam's unlawful detention and execution, as well as her relentless effort to share the experiences of Iranian women after the Islamic revolution.

Expanding the latter component, Annette Kuhn has suggested that the multivocal central character of a film, in this case *My Stolen Revolution*, positions the film as a 'memory text', and like all memory texts, it does not lead to the 'ultimate truth, but greater knowledge' (Kuhn 2002: 6). This special characteristic of the memory text is confirmed when, once the women's joint meeting has begun, it becomes clear that Persson Sarvestani, rather than participate, can in fact only listen and ask questions as the women start telling *their* stories. These five women go on to share unique memories and experiences of certain locale and situations to which the filmmaker herself cannot at all connect, let alone add to. The film's immediate narrative consequently does not become personal and subjective in relation to the filmmaker per se until its voice-over narration is added. More to the point, the multivocal testimonies of the Iranian women in *My Stolen Revolution* outweigh Persson Sarvestani's effort at visual self-inscription as the film's author by calling to mind 'the collective nature of the activity of remembering' (Kuhn 2002: 6). By narratively suggesting a certain common authorial divestiture, the film's general narrative thus clearly works against this well-defined, extra-textual authorial figure, put in place by Laura Rascaroli as a necessary point of origin and constant reference in the essay film (Rascaroli 2009).

Consequently, the insertion of an emblematic image of Persson Sarvestani in deep thought with her back turned to the spectator plays an important role to reinstall her as the film's enunciator. Her thinking pose confirms that the film's topic and interpellative qualities are exponents of *her* authorship (her masterminding) despite the women's depositions, and thus allow the enunciator to retain her hold over the film. This means that regardless of the blatant discrepancy between voice-over and screen narrative in *both* filmic fabrics, Persson Sarvestani's Self manages to remain central to the films' narratives. Pitiful or not, this line of action is thought-provoking in that it underlines the liquid nature of the multilayered film fabric in relation to the outright subjective character of her work as an auteur. By thus editing the films, Persson Sarvestani furthermore challenges the viewer's expectations of her performative intervention in them and exposes their high level of subjective interpellation.

These unexpected interventions in the films' initial narratives severely test Persson Sarvestani's authorial role in her work, placing her authorship on a par with a notion that Rascaroli has described as a 'double presence' or 'self-reflexive split' in relation to the film format. According to Rascaroli, it results in the film's authorship being disturbed and 'played out in the interstices between narrator and enunciator' (Rascaroli 2009: 40). Persson Sarvestani's 'self-reflexive split' is clearly indicated by the inconsistencies in the dialogues between her and Farah Pahlavi, as well as those between her and the five former political prisoners, in relation to the more personal topics announced to the spectator in the films' initial footage and continuous voice-over. From an epistemological point of view, Persson Sarvestani's modus operandi leads to a narrative displacement even though she must initially have been aware of the fact that she would not, for example, be able to testify to the horrors of Iran's post-revolutionary regime when inviting the women to talk about their hardship in prison in *My Stolen Revolution*.

Her interpellative authorship is therefore primarily located *outside* the films' liquid fabula and limited to her role as the film's narrator (in the form of a voice-over) and director, reminding us of the fact that 'the voice-over [is a] privileged site of the textual construction of the enunciator; and ... an instrument of expression of the author's subjectivity and thought' (Rascaroli 2009: 14).

The liquid quality of the narrative development in Persson Sarvestani's films is thus formally framed by Cecilia Sayad's notion of 'authorial divestiture', which reflects a conscious transition from traditional auteurism to a collective form of authorship (Sayad 2013: 40–41). This inclination is also suggested by Persson Sarvestani's use of *interior* interpellation (or interior monologue, resulting in the film's voice-over) as a decisive contributing factor to both films' *fabula*. Clearly, such a polyvocal variety of interpellations leaves the spectator in limbo and may diminish the authorial control over the voice-over's narrative. I would even venture to say that the reiteration of the fabula in both *The Queen and I* and *My Stolen Revolution* in fact depends on a liquid form of interpellation that risks overriding the films' efforts to present two works by a strong enunciator. By allowing the voice-over to compete with – even at time defy – the films' narratives, Persson Sarvestani risks divesting the *fabula* of her own authorial presence.

I suggest that this is a key characteristic of Persson Sarvestani's first two essay films and thus has a pivotal effect on her role as the films' enunciator and author. It also seems to have had a direct bearing on her approach to the reiteration of evidence in the form of narrative voice-over and edited filmed footage in her self-reflexive documentary practice during these years. Such a modus operandi results in a form of authorial intervention which constitutes a unique take on the essay film format. Considered the most autobiographical format in relation to Rascaroli's postulation that '[i]n first-person cinema, the address is unmistakably characterised as personal, as coming from an enunciator that overtly identifies with the empirical author' (Rascaroli 2009: 15), the impetus to introduce Nahid Persson Sarvestani as a *strong enunciator* is severely tested in the light of her authorial surrender to Farah Pahlavi in *The Queen and I*.

It is true that documentary films in the essay mode represent a hybrid form between fiction and non-fiction cinema, which results in discursive in-betweenness. What makes Persson

Sarvestani's essay films unique is subsequently their fluidity, their way of setting new targets in play, leading to a form of authorial divestiture which confirms the outright self-reflexive and liquid character of their mode. Her female authorship consequently makes way for the *liquid enunciator* in line with Zygmunt Bauman's ideas on liquid modernity as fragmented, unstable and ambivalent (see Bauman 2000). I propose that Laura Rascaroli's definition of the enunciator's different roles, in tandem with Cecilia Sayad's notions of authorial divestiture and collective authorship, all echo Bauman's suggestion that a person can shift from one social position to another in a fluid manner. Hence my call for a definition of Persson Sarvestani's performed authorship in *My Stolen Revolution* as communicated by a *liquid* enunciator, as the narrative relates to a group of women's joint journey of factual, political and intellectual discovery.

I thus posit that contrary to many other first-person filmmakers mentioned in scholarly texts, the divested authorship introduced in the films under discussion in this section may be seen as a challenge to Rascaroli's call for a *strong enunciator*, based on her suggestion that 'they [should] create a stronger impression of authorial presence than that to be experienced in most classical and narrative films.' (Rascaroli 2009: 14). Should we see Persson Sarvestani's predilection for a divested form of auteurism as openly undermining traditionally heroic properties of the enunciator as a heavenly inspired genius with consummate power? Or could it be that she endorses a possible discursive weakening of the enunciator's role by making the auteur look ambivalent in her documentaries dealing with women's political engagement in international resistance towards an extremist regime? This weakening of the enunciator's role is no doubt textually manifested by the films' liquid narratives and unstable self-reflexivity, and obviously risk lessening their affinity with the traditional idea of signature auteur products by filmmakers with a strong, personal artistic vision. And yet, this is the hallmark of Persson Sarvestani's textual agency as a political documentarist during the 2010s: 'If many documentarians seek an objective reality waiting to be unveiled, self-reflexive approaches present the director as the agent *interfering* with a purported reality; rather than simply revealing it' (Sayad 2013: 103, my italics).

By imposing a more contemporary reading of *authorial divestiture*, this theoretical framework consequently embraces both the current tenets of subjective filmmaking and hints to Persson Sarvestani's continued documentary activism in the 2020s.

PART THREE

Authorial divestiture in the twenty-first century

- *Be My Voice* (2021)
- *Son of a Mullah* (2023)

Introduction

When Nahid Persson Sarvestani returns to political filmmaking on Iranian subject matter in 2020, the conditions for documentary film production have changed profoundly. The main reason for this change is the growing dominance and international spread of digital media and especially social media and streaming channels such as YouTube.

In his excellent overview of the internationally expanded documentary activism performed through vernacular online video practice and its relation to traditional documentary media-making, including the apparatus itself, Jihoon Kim basically argues that since the 2010s, a new ecosystem of documentary media has evolved, 'characterized by the multilayered influences of citizens, mainstream media, and activists and professional documentarians' (Kim 2022: 185). The by now almost fully developed professionalisation of vernacular online video-making has been pivotal when it comes to the 'witnessing, documenting and advocating of the political events that call for participation and solidarity' (Kim 2022: 185). Although Kim leaves political events in Iran factually to one side, I argue that his discussion of this general technical and aesthetic transition in the documentary media landscape is fully relevant for my purposes, discussions and conclusions in relation to Persson Sarvestani's documentary production on Iranian subject matter in the 2020s.[1]

Citizen-camera-witnessing videos have also had an increasing impact on severely monitored societies such as Iran, and they thus provide important counter-narratives about their society by underpinning both the making and sharing of underground documentaries. In tandem with this evolution, handheld devices such as mobile phones are characterised by increased technical performance, as well as being used more frequently among members of societies all over the world. Thus equipped, ordinary Iranians have had increased means to testify and remediate life in Iran to the outside world, and all these facts have contributed to an increased impression of authorial divestiture as far as documentary filmmaking is concerned. Andrew Chadwick has neatly framed this change towards a more hybrid media landscape:

> The hybrid media system is built upon interactions among older and newer media logics—where logics are defined as technologies, genres, norms, behaviors, and organizational forms—in the reflexively connected fields of media and politics. Actors in this system are articulated by complex and ever-evolving relationships based upon adaptation and interdependence and simultaneous concentrations and diffusions of power. Actors create, tap, or steer information flows in ways that suit their goals and in ways that modify, enable, or disable the agency of others, across and between a range of older and newer media settings. (Chadwick 2017: 4)

Consequently, Jihoon Kim points out that all three different areas of documentary practice have been directly affected by

---

[1] Kim mainly provides examples from the Arab spring (2010–2013) in Tunisia, Egypt and Libya; the Gezi Park protests in Turkey (2013); Hong Kong's Umbrella Movement (2014) and the 2019–2020 protests against the Extradition Bill; and the two waves of Black Lives Matter in the United States (2014 and 2020).

this changed media landscape: production, distribution and consumption (Kim 2022: 191). Regardless of whether the product is a protest-oriented online video, or an activist film/video, or a traditional documentary, the transmedia strategies involved in its production, distribution and consumption share similarities that encourage further proximity in their study. Kim bases his conclusion on the argument that:

> [V]ernacular online videos for documenting and provoking social change signal an *expansion* of the activist documentary's *subject*. For these demonstrate that ordinary citizens have been endowed with the behaviors of witnessing, documenting, and distributing that were hitherto assigned to filmmakers, journalists, and activists. This also entails an expansion of activist documentary's *media* and *artifact*, inasmuch as the amateur online videos produced and circulated by ordinary citizens have functioned to represent, articulate, and mobilize bodies and voices of the subjects who engaged in the movements for social justice and change, and of those who were victimized by political suppression and injustice. Since the videos take on several technical and aesthetic features of activist film and video, their distance from politically committed professional nonfiction media practices has been so diminished that there have been dynamic overlaps and influences between the two in both online and offline scenes of protests. (Kim 2022: 192, italics in original)

While still funded by Swedish Television, the new digital affordances as well as the publicising of documentary footage play a significant role in the discourse in Persson Sarvestani's political documentaries in the 2020s, resulting in yet new approaches to her subject matter in both *Be My Voice* (2021) and *Son of a Mullah* (2023).

By way of introduction, Kim presents two important references to historical feminist activist documentary contributions that are pivotal and hark back to my introductory discussion of the director's work on this topic. He writes that, although embedded in different layers of late 1960s Western radicalism, one of the fundamental goals at the time, as well as for today's expanded documentary activism, is activist documentary cinema's 'capacity to record, provoke, and persuade in favor of creating collective consciousness, engagement, and solidarity' (Kim 2022: 200). The feminist movement's documentaries on women's conditions, discussed in Chapters 1 and 2 of this book, had the same objective and are hence again considered pivotal to the overall development of women's rights in the Western world. Kim writes:

> The feminist wave in the 1970s ... amplified the activist aesthetic of documentary ... while also leading to a new breed of documentary films whose rhetorical strategies of self-expression linked the personal explorations of women ... to the political critique of patriarchal ... norms. (Kim 2022: 187)

Revisiting notions such as Jane M. Gaines' 'political mimesis' is helpful to explicate the development of expanded documentary activism. Originally introduced in 1999, Gaines presented the concept of 'political mimesis' as footage 'address[ing] what it is that the committed documentary wants us to do' (Gaines 1999: 90). These are films that 'make audience members want to kick and yell, film that make them want to do something *because of the conditions in the world of the audience*' (Renov, ibid., italics in original). Kim reminds us that '[t]he aesthetic of political mimesis in the contexts of global protests has been amplified, partly because citizen-camera-witnessing videos produced on their sites aim to encourage viewers to identify with and participate in the same struggle as that of the subjects they depict' (Kim 2022: 201).

Taking the concept of 'political mimesis' one step further, I suggest that *Be My Voice* on the whole functions as an echo chamber to the extent that it also represents an act of political mimesis. There is, however, one important exception: Persson Sarvestani makes her film from the sidelines. She does not actively participate in the actions; she references them.

Another notion from 1970s radical filmmaking that is brought back into the light is Patricia Zimmermann's concept of 'on-the-ground filmmaking', 'a mode of documentary film production that portrays people occupying and struggling on and for social spaces [and] the filmmaker's interaction with them' (Kim 2022: 201). As far as Zimmermann was concerned, the latter, physical interaction as well as the subject matter in question, expands the set-up of a traditional documentary practice by 'collaps[ing] the border between maker and subject as a false divide and depoliticized binary opposition' (Zimmermann 2000: 95). As for the act of recording itself, the filmmaking apparatus is stripped of its technological privileges and 'instead recast as a membrane, a permeable surface through which relations between and along maker and subject pass and comingle' (Ibid.). Moving her discussion of the concept she labels 'expanded subject' forward into our time, Kim argues that contemporary citizens' ubiquitous witness documentaries recorded during gatherings to perform political activities have again contributed to such a shift in the power structure of on-the-ground filmmaking, by popularising the use of the camera as 'membrane' (Kim 2022: 201). As we shall see, this development of the documentary apparatus is key to my discussions of the changed cinematic fabric in Persson Sarvestani's documentaries in this chapter.

The other implication directly related to arguments presented in relation to Persson Sarvestani's work in this part of the book is Kim's discussion of the effect of vernacular online documentary videos on traditional documentary strategies and how this leads to a yet more poignant form of authorial divestiture, partially intimated in my above discussion of *My Stolen Revolution*:

> I would argue that the various vernacular online videos responding to the global protests suggest that the boundaries between documentary filmmaking and other nonfiction media practices, and between the professional and the amateur, have ostensibly become porous to the extent that these two practices have *shared* their performative claim to the real. (Kim 2022: 205, my italics)

Regarding their reception, the distribution of filmed documentaries is no longer limited to theatrical exhibitions alone; instead, they reach many more spectators around the world via different streaming techniques. Both films have also entered the traditional film festival circuits, but as yet with surprisingly limited success. *Be My Voice* was in 2021–2022 nominated four times at the Göteborg Film Festival, Cinema for Peace Awards, Millennium Docs Against Gravity, and Tempo Documentary Festival. *Son of a Mullah* was nominated twice in 2024, at the Krakow Film Festival and Guldbagge Awards (Sweden).

5

Expanding her documentary apparatus: *Be My Voice* (2021)

The continued articulations of civil unrest in Iran in the 2010s compelled Nahid Persson Sarvestani to remain vigilant and resolute in her documentary practice:

> The Iranian authorities' extreme callousness towards its people during the outpour of social unrest during the election in 2009 enhanced my urge to interact with the reported civil abuse. I had seen in the media, a new generation – not least of young, courageous women – taking the lead against the regime in the streets, thus risking arrest, prison, and death. (Persson Sarvestani 2011: 297, my translation)

The director's new, expanded documentary practice of the 2020s is currently geared towards close collaborations with political activists in the West for the Iranian cause. In her first political documentary of the 2020s, *Be My Voice*, I suggest that she thus takes on the role of acting 'membrane' when she makes a portrait film about the Iranian American activist Masih Alinejad. In this film, the director too is fully inscribed in the frame, sometimes as Alinejad's discussant, but more often simply her shadow or sidekick. My discussion of this film thus revolves around two major themes: first, the performance of authorial divestiture in relation to Patricia R. Zimmermann's 'membrane' concept (Zimmermann 2000). I shall also be discussing the relation between the film's excerpts and the tenets of the aesthetic characteristics of the contemporary form of expanded activist documentary cinema, as presented by Jihoon Kim (2022).

Be My Voice, the film's title, was originally the hashtag used for one of Masih Alinejad's campaigns on Instagram to empower young Iranians' resistance to the regime. Alinejad is an Iranian human rights activist, refugee and journalist who has been active in the United States during the past ten years. Using social media as her political weapon, Alinejad also initiated 'White Wednesdays' as a way for young Iranian women to demonstrate against the law of mandatory veiling. The response from the Iranian public has been overwhelming and Alinejad receives many thousand messages per day from her followers, placing her under enormous pressure to act for them while putting herself in political peril. Using traditional production routines for digital TV broadcasts, Alinejad also presents a weekly public broadcast in which she comments on Iranian affairs.

In terms of *political discourse*, the documentary narrative in *Be My Voice* essentially revolves around women's issues, with joint discussions and republicised visual coverage of the 'White Wednesday' campaign inside and outside Iran as the main visual imagery. The narrative slightly changes direction towards the end of the film. Following Alinejad's online monitoring of events in Iran, her news feed is then suddenly immersed with viral messages related to the unseemly rise of national fuel prices late in 2019. The social unrest is vast, but still sidelined by the news that Alinejad's and Persson Sarvestani's friend and colleague Rohollo Zam has been kidnapped and brought back to Iran. The film's narrative ends in 2020 with the news that Zam has been executed by the Iranian government, followed by Persson Sarvestani's insertion of mixed, contemporary activist and archival footage from the 1980s of women marching for their rights in Iran.

The documentary footage of *Be My Voice* shows Persson Sarvestani accompanying Alinejad in her everyday life and was shot in intervals over a period of time, in what seems to be New York. The film's narrative reflects a chronological order of events in the TV presenter's professional life during Persson Sarvestani's visits. Working diachronically, that narrative thread is intertwined with inserted footage from home videos and photos to provide information about Alinejad's background and life as a young girl in Iran. In addition to these private images, the spectator is also presented with vernacular activist documentary footage and photos exhibiting later political subject matter in contemporary Iran. The director addresses the spectator via voice-over as usual but in this documentary, Persson Sarvestani, very importantly, speaks in *Persian*, not in Swedish. I suggest her change of voice-over language is the direct result of her general turn to a production mode more in tune with expanded documentary activism, opting for *Persian* mainly with its distribution to a larger audience in mind.

The first example of how a more hybrid media system has impacted on the production mode and film fabric of Persson Sarvestani's political documentaries in the 2020s is thus clearly visible in *Be My Voice*. The film is set up around three different types of documentary sources: compiled vernacular amateur footage, archival footage and photos, and contemporary footage portraying Masih Alinejad recorded and edited by Persson Sarvestani herself in her hometown, as well as abroad. To complicate the theoretical unpacking of the film further, the relation between these types of documentary material is consistent and porous throughout the film, intimating that the director's choice to allow a heavily expanded media landscape to affect its discourse is a conscious choice of authorial approach, as we shall see.

To begin with, the most pertinent change in documentary source material is the vast amount of online activist footage driving and even determining the narrative discourse in *Be My Voice*. Portions of this footage were recorded directly from Alinejad's handheld devices. These short, sometimes clandestinely produced, amateur clips stand in clear contrast to Persson Sarvestani's organised filming of Alinejad's daily life by being blurry, rushed and offering mainly shaky visuality. Jihoon Kim, in discussing the range of aesthetic characteristics of activist citizens' vernacular documentary footage, mentions two categories that apply to the type of footage shown in *Be My Voice*: 'witness videos' and 'documentation videos'. The first category 'offer[s] caught-on-camera records of socially or politically unjust conditions, police or military brutality, and human rights violations' (Kim 2022: 195). The second category relates to 'people's marches and other acts of civil obedience, their oral testimonies or speeches, community meetings, and performances to promote collective identity and to create a sense of solidarity and belonging' (Kim 2022: 195–196). Both categories deal with the activism on citizens' rights, around which the main narrative in *Be My Voice* revolves.

And yet, the film first and foremost chronicles Masih Alinejad's role as an exiled advocate for human rights issues related to Iran in the very late 2010s, which is to say just before the Covid-19 pandemic. In terms of point of view, this footage again relies on Persson Sarvestani being fully inscribed in the frame as Alinejad's companion, much like the role she had in *The Queen and I*. What is surprising is the almost complete lack of conversations around political matters between the two women. The documentary instead chronicles Alinejad's extremely stressful everyday life and work, forcing Persson Sarvestani to ask Alinejad's husband, Kambiz Foroohar, how she really copes with the heavy demand on her engagement from all corners of society. When the two women talk together, it is primarily to reminiscence around pre-revolutionary memories of life in Iran. Their avoidance of open conversations about the political situation in Iran thus transposes that discursive trajectory of the documentary's narrative to rely on its imagery, placing its contents and meaning in the hands of the audience to be discussed and analysed.

Persson Sarvestani's insertion of a second exterior documentary source, in the form of archival footage and photos of Alinejad as a young girl in the remote Iranian village where she grew up, adds a third discursive layer to the film. Reiterating important parts of her early life, as well as the current relationship with her family still living in Iran, helps position and explain why Alinejad has become a central figure among the Iranian diasporas. Embracing the cool objectivity of traditional documentary discourse, this archive material also provides an important background to and understanding of Alinejad's political activism. There is, for instance, an interesting excerpt from the Iranian countryside in the late 1990s, in which Alinejad is goading her peasant father into letting her drive the tractor. This scene was probably documented just for fun, but her father's fierce refusal, saying 'it would be wrong' if she was to drive it, is presented as an instance where Iranian men demonstrate their adherence to the patriarchal order still ruling Iranian society. While this type of home movie and family photos represents a completely different form of documentary source both visually and discursively, this material contributes important historical background information by explaining Alinejad's present engagement and political activism as well as concurring with the bottom line of the contemporary online documentary activism remediated in the film.

The political voice of a documentary like *Be My Voice* thus remediates a dual thematic emphasis: that of social issues working in tandem with a personal portraiture, by many considered to be the two most important realms in documentary film practice. According to Bill Nichols this is because 'it is in the interrelationship between the individual and the society that questions of power and hierarchy, ideology and politics stand most forcefully revealed' (Nichols 2010: 249). Resulting in an effective hybrid form, such a combination of topics excludes a binary labelling (what Nichols calls 'a black-and-white choice') of the documentary as either expository *or* observational/participatory, as each mode approaches the realm of political engagement from a distinct angle (Nichols 2001: 248–249). Instead, both emphases 'proliferate across the full range of documentary representation', but it should be remembered that 'the individual's primary importance is what they can tell us about the larger issue' (Nichols 2001: 243). In connection with the rise of #BlackLivesMatter and Hong Kong's #UmbrellaRevolution, An Xiao Mina contends that:

> The internet was essential to the rise of both movements. It made them visible to themselves and to each other. It's nearly impossible now to think of a social movement without the internet, and as the world comes online, communities advocating for change are popping up globally, in places large and small, channeling their energies to the streets and to the web. (Mina 2019: 3)

This observation gives me reason to return to Patricia R. Zimmermann's notion regarding the documentary apparatus in play in 'films-on-the-ground' appearing in *Be My Voice*. I suggest that the camera's role as a membrane – 'the borders between maker and subject, active agents and representations dissolve into a more fluid, permeable construct' – very precisely characterises how we could interpret the 'witness' and 'documentation' excerpts in Persson Sarvestani's film (Zimmermann 2000: 95). The divestment of the traditional documentarist's privileged position and one-on-one interaction with the documentary subject is further emphasised by the fact that many excerpts of activist documentary footage remediated in *Be My Voice* were recorded at a distance, embracing a point of view which not only includes the performing subject but also other individuals in the crowd filming the event in equal measure – and most probably with the same intent. By representing a form of expanded and highly effective mode of participatory documentary, the question begging to be asked of these discursively identical excerpts is what effect a compilation of *multiple membranes* has on the reception of a political or activist action recorded under such circumstances. I thus posit that other than increasing its role as visible evidence, a large crowd's unanimous effort to record a certain political event taking place in a local public sphere increases each excerpt's ability to raise public awareness on multiple levels elsewhere, when circulated widely as *participatory media*.

Nichols' and Zimmermann's claims regarding the general effects of a reduced apparatus in favour of a more fluid type of documentary authorship are furthermore relevant for my discussion of *Be My Voice* on two levels, the cinematic and the discursive. I have addressed the former level in my above exposé of the film's different types of footage and still images, pointing out that these documentary sources are intermingled, partly through remediation, throughout Persson Sarvestani's film. I now move on to discuss its imprint on the film's discursive level.

Documentary strategies in *Be My Voice*

Emblematic images in transition

The privately filmed, sometimes serenely set, scenes of unveiling in *Be My Voice* physically mimic the silent pantomimes performed for the camera in *My Stolen Revolution*. Those short clips filmed by the individual woman herself in privacy, at home, in a garden or in the street at night, represent the major form of emblematic images in the 2021 film. Their ritualised form verges on the symbolic, which I consider to here be emblematic as the clips typically present the act of unveiling either in silence as a pantomime or accompanied by a short speech. Intellectually compelling, a common trait of these short films is that they come across as very controlled and somehow 'objective', some of them even paying attention to such technicalities as the lighting. Through the act of filming and sharing the clip with Masih Alinejad, these women show their heartfelt wish for change.

Over time, these witness documentaries made for 'White Wednesdays', however, came to include a different visual aesthetic, indicating both a performative and documentary transition of the act. The pronounced emblematic character of the early 'White Wednesday' videos here transcends into 'documentation videos', recorded in crowds gathered around a woman publicly unveiling herself. For natural reasons, these participatory documentary videos, besides being constricted by shaky camera movements and insufficient lighting, above all reflect impressions of hypermobility and affectivity. Kim references 'hypermobility' as 'the photographer's chaotic movement of filming that leads to [its cinematic impression of] tension and directedness and aimlessness' (Kim 2022: 199). The second characteristic, affectivity, responds to the film's embeddedness in 'the creation of emotions as source of authenticity in contrast to conventional journalism's pursuit of objectivity' (Kim, ibid.). Admittedly, these are characteristics that make these videos more visually effective while at the same time contributing increased political urgency by being self-referential and embedded.

What is worth noticing about the compiled form of mobilisation videos in *Be My Voice* is the visual effect of their dominating aesthetic of amateurish rawness and urgency compared to the emblematic images typical of Persson Sarvestani's previous documentary authorship. Kim characterises this aesthetic as akin to that of direct cinema in terms of shaky camera and dependence on natural, often insufficient light, attesting to 'the videographer's conscious filming for collective witness, identification and solidarity' (Kim, ibid.). I hold that including excerpts characterised by political urgency rather than reflective serenity, as well as participatory filmmaking rather than individual directorship, generally attests to the documentary transition of Persson Sarvestani's filmmaking. Neither of these characteristics have been previously found in Persson Sarvestani's documentary film practice. Making use of its embeddedness and urgency, however, immediately echoes Jane M. Gaines' notion of 'political mimesis', encouraging public action among both practitioners and audiences.

It seems that Masih Alinejad's call for similar types of footage, currently referred to as *participatory media*, celebrating 'White Wednesdays', resulted in both 'witnessing' and 'documentation' videos. Portions of them are remediated in compiled sequences in *Be My Voice*, beginning with the most emblematic ones. Even so, seen as a whole, they all engage with the same issue, which begs the question of whether this type of expanded documentary activism also accommodates a new conceptual mode, akin to the definition of an internet meme. Limor Shifman has identified the internet meme as:

> (a) a group of digital items sharing common characteristics of content, form, and/or stance, which
> (b) were created with awareness of each other, and
> (c) were circulated, imitated, and/or transformed via the Internet by many users. (Shifman 2014: 41)

Shifman later goes on to define three common characteristics of the internet-based political meme:

> (1) Memes as forms of persuasion or political advocacy.
> (2) Memes as a grassroots action.
> (3) Memes as modes of expression and public discussion.

(Shifman 2014: 122–123)

A pertinent example confirming a labelling of the 'White Wednesday' clips as political memes is the so-called pussyhats worn by the protesters in the Many Women's March in New York, and many other parts around the world, in 2017. An Xiao Mina asserts that:

> On [Donald Trump's] Inauguration Day and the day of protests that followed it, countless selfies of people in … pink pussyhats flooded social media feeds. Each selfie was slightly different – sometimes in a group, sometimes in solitude; sometimes on the streets, sometimes at home; people of many genders, races, and ages. But the symbolism was the same and – for better or worse – became a feature of the protests and a signal to supporters and the broader community; this is who I am, and this is what I stand for.

(Mina 2019: 5)

If this assumption is correct, the earlier forms of emblematic images representing 'accented' notions of nostalgia and loss, as well as authorial fortitude, similar to those in my above discussion of *The Queen and I*, are altogether replaced in *Be My Voice*. According to Shifman's above sets of characteristics for political memes, Nahid Persson Sarvestani's documentary practice instead took on the role of being a membrane echoing a more pronounced political and activist character.

Mise-en-abîme in a secondary frame

In *Be My Voice*, Persson Sarvestani again expands the documentary narrative through use of *mise-en-abîme*. The visual displays of such video clips are, however, in many ways representative of a different form of film-in-the-film experience compared to the pantomimes discussed in *My Stolen Revolution*. Unlike those sequences, the clips in *Be My Voice* were not directed or even initiated by Persson Sarvestani herself but by other, largely unknown, people.

Unlike the pantos which were seamlessly embedded in the overall film fabric, the film-in-the-film sequences in *Be My Voice* are clearly exhibited on Alinejad's digital devices. By filming them, Persson Sarvestani remediates the clips through her documentary apparatus, which results in their content being placed within a secondary frame, from both a discursive and visual point of view.

The clips are physically presented as having a visual frame from a secondary device beyond the film frame itself. Yacavone notes that 'different devices may be part of the same reflexive forms' when appearing in the same film product. The reflexive function of a film-in-the-film is normally considered to be either formal or political (Yacavone 2023: 106). Presenting it in transmedial form, in this case through a process of remediation, as originating from a secondary screen device, does not ontologically impair its

Figure 5.1 *Mise-en-abîme* in a secondary frame in *Be My Voice*. Screenshot by author.

merit as visible evidence. From a discursive point of view, film-in-the-film components characterised by allusive/intertextual reflexivity, such as the remediated video clips in *Be My Voice*, retain their full awareness-making potential (Yacavone 2023: 107). They contribute pivotal knowledge to the film's overall narrative and must thus be considered as contributing elements of meta-cinema to Persson Sarvestani's film, regardless of them being left uncommented on by the voice-over. According to Bill Nichols, '[r]eflexivity and consciousness-raising go hand in hand' in that

> ideological constraints can be juxtaposed with alternative positions and subjectivities, affinities and relations of production, precisely as the feminist documentary has done. As a political concept, reflexivity grounds itself in the materiality of representation but turns, or returns, the viewer beyond the text, to those material practices that inform the body politic (Nichols 1991: 67).

I here read the 'materialisms' and 'body politic' mentioned by Nichols as fully connected to the role of progressive political activism and citizen documentaries I discuss in connection with especially Patricia Zimmermann's scholarly work.

To sum up, I hold that the appearance of film-in-the-film sequences in Persson Sarvestani's oeuvre represents a designated form of political reflexivity and should be understood as a fully acknowledged 'utterance' by an enunciative authority to the spectator.

Divested authorship

The overall discursive development in *Be My Voice* indicates an expanded move towards authorial divestiture since its genesis in *My Stolen Revolution*. In the former film, Persson Sarvestani's conscious transition from auteurism to collective authorship and a more liquid form of political activism is demonstrated from the very onset through her choice of documentary 'twin' subject.

Like the director, Masih Alinejad is also a political journalist and activist invested in subject matter pertaining to human rights issues in post-revolutionary Iran. Recording Alinejad's day-to-day life and work thus naturally leads to a divested form of authorship. Elaborating on her suggested notion, Cecilia Sayad goes on to suggest that such an authorial divestiture transforms the auteur (using Jean-Luc Godard as her example) into a mere *vessel*. The term vessel carries with it a distinct reference to Romanticism and the idea of the genius as a mere receptor of divine inspiration that must take physical form. Such a stale and precursory approach to the notion is, however, quite unsuitable in relation to Persson Sarvestani's contemporary documentary practice, although Godard did indeed 'direct' several productions in collaboration with the Dziga Vertov Group, adhering to a materialist type of filmmaking and editing the shots into a final film product. Having the films scholarly presented and studied as examples of 1970s 'materialist filmmaking' is as a matter of fact based on the assumption that they are first and foremost *political*, leaving all notions of Romantic auteurism to the side.

What is more relevant to my study is Patricia Zimmermann's idea of the technical apparatus under authorial control (vessel) turning into an authorially divested *membrane* representing an echo system working in tandem with an expanded media landscape. In Persson Sarvestani's case, such a transposition of authorship implies that her recent documentary practice is polyvocal and relying on the input of, for instance, documentary footage contributed by other documentary subjects. Cecilia Sayad has suggested that by thus discursively multiplying the authorial voice, the auteur makes others speak for herself (Sayad 2013: 40–41). On the other hand, it also means that through her use of a more fluid authorial documentary practice, Nahid Persson Sarvestani's films voice the opinions of many, many women, and not just herself. As for her role as the film's enunciator, I urge the reader to see that Persson Sarvestani is still positioned at the side, not centre stage, of the events taking place. As a political documentary, *Be My Voice* is therefore in its entirety a membrane.

6

Polyvocal political activism as a matrix for the liquid documentary: *Son of a Mullah* (2023)

Introduction

In *Son of a Mullah*, Nahid Persson Sarvestani hones her discursively multivocal authorial voice further while at the same time placing herself *in media res*. When I wrote earlier that the documentary discourse in *Be My Voice* mainly *references* 'political mimesis', I referred to the fact that the director did not personally engage in the ongoing political activities. She remediated them by channelling Masih Alinejad's activist practice and excerpts from online documentary activism through the membrane of her own film camera to form a political discourse. In *Son of a Mullah*, she performs on-the-ground filmmaking by redressing her role as an investigating reporter in situ. This was an utterly daring step to take physically as the increased political activism involved brings the documentary topic into high gear right from the start.

> The regime does everything to harm political activists, so one must be careful. Avi

By way of introduction, the first minutes of the film are spent presenting the most influential Iranian news anchors and their internationally broadcasted programmes informing the world about the political situation in Iran. Persson Sarvestani's voice-over narrative is again presented in Swedish in *Son of a Mullah*. This introductory sequence is intercut with several layers of remediated online activist documentary footage of confrontations between the Iranian security forces and domestic protesters. Masih Alinejad is presented as one among these TV personalities, and so is Rohollo Zam, who is already familiar to the spectator who has seen *Be My Voice*. The production chronology of *Son of a Mullah* is, however, reversed, in the sense that Persson Sarvestani's curiosity about why the son of an Iranian high priest had rejected his life of luxury and started working for the opposition had led her to begin documenting Zam and his news channel in France before she made *Be My Voice*. The production of the film we now know as *Son of a Mullah* runs from early 2019 to 2023. It came to a temporary halt when Zam was unexpectedly kidnapped in Iraq in 2019. The subsequent official Iranian broadcasting of Zam's trials, the TV programmes about him and the officially declared death sentence leading up to his execution in early 2020 drove Persson Sarvestani to carry on with the film about him and his colleagues. Hence, the film's discourse branches out and contains documentary evidence of the Iranian authorities' involvement in the hoax that cost Zam his life, but also his daughter's political engagement in France in the early months of 2023. The documentary narrative is thus twofold, revolving around events taking place before and after Rohollo Zam's death. It also explains why some of the 2019 footage related to Zam, his family and work situation in France included in *Be My Voice* is repeated in *Son of a Mullah*.

Rohollo Zam was born just after the Islamic revolution in Iran in 1979 and grew up in a deeply religious family with close ties to the new regime. His father was a mullah and part of the Iranian government. Zam's disappointment in the country's increasing religious dictatorship turned him into a political dissident, and he left the country after serving a short jail sentence in the 1990s. Together with his wife he took up residency in France, and started his own news channel, Amad News. Like his colleague Avi Javanmardi of AVA Today, he specialised in revealing the corruption and money laundering among the clerical elite in Iran, revealing the country's development into a kleptocracy that was partly in response to the increased economic sanctions from Western countries. There are plenty of global, digital news channels run by exiled Iranians, broadcasting and debating Iranian news like this around the clock. Like many other journalists and private citizens with an interest in Iranian affairs, Persson Sarvestani follows this news on a daily, sometimes hourly basis. To represent visible evidence contributing to the political discourse in *Son of a Mullah*, the filmmaker incessantly remediates news footage pertaining to not only official news broadcasts but also conversations between the different documentary subjects. Edited in a montage form, these sometimes very short clips represent an important contributing component to the film's overall intricate, fast-paced and almost unbelievable documentary narrative.

To help the onlooker navigate through the film's complicated chronology, *Son of a Mullah* was also edited with time captions indicating the place and/or year a certain event took place. As for the broadcasts from Iranian TV, they were all remediated from digital sources. I list the events in which the director herself took part here, briefly referencing their contents:

'Sweden, December 2018'

A clip from the director's initial contact with Rohollo Zam, voicing her interest in making a documentary about him. They have apparently never met or been involved with one another professionally before. Zam, however, knows of her film *The Queen and I*. He agrees to her suggestion. This footage of her professional activities is intercut with imagery of the surrounding landscape, indicating that the director is at home, working in her office. This by now well-known mix of personal and professional footage confirms the porous line between enunciator and author in Persson Sarvestani's documentary practice.

'France, January 2019'

The director goes to France to stay with Zam and his family for a few weeks. Zam has police protection, which means that leaving the house is very complicated. Persson Sarvestani, for the first time, interviews her documentary subject in a traditional style about the character of his work, and monitors it daily for the camera. This section of *Son of a Mullah* was thus recorded in a clearly expository manner, bringing the audience up to speed about dissident journalism and the working conditions that apply. On this topic, Zam claims to have led the demonstrations in Iran in 2017 from his desk in France. He also tells the director about his childhood and adolescence in Iran, how his political engagement led to imprisonment and his subsequent exile in France. Zam willingly answers all Persson Sarvestani's questions and comes across as very self-confident in relation to his professional standing, boasting about his access to inside information in high places, his personal administrator 'Shirin' and the importance of his work in exposing the general corruption in the Iranian government. According to Zam, there are several indications that the Iranian leadership is very annoyed with his many 'scoops', and he receives death threats on a daily basis. He is occupied with finding the economic funding to continue his work via televised broadcasting, instead of communicating digitally via his phone. He intimates that an exiled Iranian man in Australia has offered to fund his TV channel if he moves there.

The presentation of this section of *Son of a Mullah* is crosscut with remediated online imagery, as well as the director's more intimate footage portraying different members of the Zam family and their everyday life. The documentary mode in these instances is observational yet immersed. The director's relationship to the camera and her documentary subject in the latter sequences thus remind me of that in *Prostitution Behind the Veil*, in which she is also the only camera person. There is, on the other hand, an interesting tension between Rohollo Zam operating securely from inside *huis clos*, interacting with highly dangerous real-life events only at a distance. These somehow 'safe' conditions necessarily inform the director's balanced and unhurried documentary recording in this sequence as well.

From a visual point of view, the documentary footage in this section partly resembles that in *Be My Voice*, which is to say it chronicles and closely follows Zam in his everyday life both privately and professionally.

'Kurdistan' – no date

During Persson Sarvestani's stay with the Zam family in France, Rohollo Zam is in almost daily contact with a colleague who at first does not want to be introduced to the director. Once he understands who she is and the documentary topic of her project, she is invited to meet him somewhere in Kurdistan. He is Avi Javanmardi of AVA News, an American Iranian journalist operating in the open, surrounded by advanced security, since he has been subject to several assassination attempts over the years. Javanmardi brings her to his intelligence unit where several staff work around the clock to follow Iranian affairs and tells her about his life as a political dissident and activist journalist. Moving on to current political events, there seems to be big funding money illegally moved from Iran on offer, but Javanmardi wants the Iranian man handling it to prove he has rightfully inherited it. Persson Sarvestani tells him about a similar offer recently made to Zam, which makes him even more suspicious.

I suggest that it is at this very moment, finding herself at the centre of his intelligence operation, that the director resumes her role as an investigating reporter in a manner which is quite unexpected for anyone following her documentary practice over time.

In the following sequences we see Persson Sarvestani sitting working on her computer among the rest of Javanmardi's team, visibly engaged in the ongoing events. Among different issues, the question of corruption in the highest echelons of the Iranian government is again on the table when she discusses the current situation with Javanmardi. Shortly afterwards, the latter makes a comment about the 'funny news' Rohollo Zam has posted over

Figure 6.1 The director as investigative journalist in *Son of a Mullah*. Screenshot by author.

the past few weeks. Could he be being manipulated by someone? They try and find out more about Zam's secretary 'Shirin'.

Upon her return to Sweden, Persson Sarvestani receives a death threat which is immediately reported to the police. A few days later, she is suddenly contacted by an anonymous person allegedly in possession of interesting secret documents which should be of interest to her. Paying the offer little notice, the director instead starts wondering how this person knows she is making a film. Setting up her camera, she has a completely incoherent conversation with an anonymous person inviting her to come and film. Relating the incidents to Zam, he warns her that she might be under threat.

'Sweden, March 2019'

Watching Iranian news at home, Persson Sarvestani is confronted with a fake documentary about Rohollo Zam using short, speech-distorted clips of comments he is supposed to have made, making him out as an infernal, vulgar and egocentric journalist, concocting false 'scoops' about Iran – a country he obviously hates – for the benefit of his own career. The 'documentary' is broadcast by Iranian Television at a time when many viewers watch and it has been produced in an obvious effort to raise suspicion among the national resistance groups towards all counter-political activists operating from outside the country. Avi Javanmardi says there is a big chance that fake documentaries like the one about Zam help the Islamist government achieve this goal. He warns the director about Zam, who is now not only professionally isolated but also working hard to regain confidence among his followers. Javanmardi is, however, certain that Zam is under serious threat from the regime and that Persson Sarvestani should avoid contacting him.

The director goes back over her documentary footage from her meetings with Zam, looking into the Australian man who contacted him, in particular. She finds it odd that all Zam's contacts are somehow linked to the regime.

Offering a narrative pause, the above sequences of Persson Sarvestani working from home are intercut with outdoor emblematic images reflecting the wintry landscape and herself in deep thought.

'October 2019'

News of Rohollo Zam is shown on Iranian Television and other news channels. Zam appears before the camera and makes (a forced) confession of his crimes. Persson Sarvestani watches the instalments from her home, realising that he must be in Iranian custody. But how did that happen?

'Tehran, February 2020'

The trial of Zam is televised by Iranian Television. He is also publicly shamed in interviews in popular actuality programmes. One interviewer tries to make him reveal his work colleagues abroad under humiliating circumstances.

The practical circumstances around Zam's kidnapping have now been clarified. Persson Sarvestani is instead pondering why he went to Iraq at all, and who made him go. She also alleges via voice-over that all the publicity around his arrest and subsequent trial is meant to discourage national counter-activism as well as casting a negative reflection on international dissident groups.

'Paris'

Persson Sarvestani goes back to Paris and contacts Zam's good friend. He tells her the whole story about how 'Shirin' made Zam go to Iraq and how he was kidnapped by the Iranian secret police immediately after he landed there.

'Tehran'

The director intercuts the footage from her visit in Paris with a short clip from a publicly broadcast Iranian TV series made about the kidnapping and subsequent trial of Rohollo Zam. His character in the series is again presented as a vulgar capitalist who has been led astray by Western values.

'Paris'

Avi Javanmardi arrives in Paris and the three of them map the entire sequence of events leading to Zam's arrest. AVA News publicises the complicated circumstances to its followers. They also manage to get an interview with 'Shirin', who all the time worked undercover for the Iranian security forces to monitor Zam and lead him into the trap. The Australian offer of a television programme was part of another effort to trap him.

This information is later confirmed by Zam's father when the director contacts him.

Stockholm (uncaptioned)

Persson Sarvestani watches a direct broadcast from the Iranian court when Zam receives his death sentence. The director again intercuts this sequence with emblematic images of the natural scenery around her house to offer the spectator a narrative pause. Going back to the news coverage, the emblematic imagery is immediately followed by the international news reports of Zam's hanging in December 2020.

This devastating footage is followed by remediated anonymous footage showing Zam's father ritually ridding himself of his clerical insignia (mullah cloak and hat) immediately after his son's burial. The father tells Persson Sarvestani about the family's last meeting with him, over the phone.

'Iran, 2022–23'

Activist documentary footage from the demonstrations organised in Iran after the murder of Mahsa Amini in September 2022. The protesters (men and women) are chanting 'Woman, Life, Freedom'.

'Paris'

Persson Sarvestani's footage from the demonstrations occurring simultaneously on the same topic in Paris. Rohollo Zam's daughter takes the stand and speaks to the crowd about gender apartheid and human rights.

Documentary strategies in *Son of a Mullah*

On balance, it is fair to say that the documentary narrative in *Son of a Mullah* is very complex, fast paced and still leaves many questions about the exact chain of events unanswered. These glitches, omissions and simplifications are, however, not meant to mislead the onlooker. Among other things, there are security measures that must be upheld for the safety of the participants.

Narrative

As already mentioned, the film's narrative is based on two major documentary sources: first, footage recorded by Persson Sarvestani herself and her team, and, second, remediated footage from digital sources. The first half of the film mainly reflects the director's effort to produce a documentary film about Rohollo Zam's decision to abandon his privileged life as the son of an Iranian mullah to work as a dissident journalist in exile, under permanent threats to his life. The production mode applied in this initial section of the film mainly resembles that used in *Be My Voice* in terms of the director's self-inscription, the mix of footage and the expository mode of documentary approach. The only differing component is basically the choice of language for the voice-over: Persian in the film about Alinejad, and Swedish for *Son of a Mullah*.

It is fair to say that the arrest of Rohollo Zam takes Persson Sarvestani's project in a completely new direction, not least because she is by then also implicated in the events. She quickly realises that the death threat she received on her return from her first visit to the Zam family means that the Iranian authorities know about her ongoings. After immediately reporting it to the Swedish police, she quickly starts to investigate *who* made them aware of her work. Who is the mole?

The second half of the film revolves around two major events. On a personal level, it brings the director's collaboration with friends and colleagues of Rohollo Zam to the fore in quickly paced sequences packed with information. Persson Sarvestani's self-inscription in these events attests to her integral and equal partnership with her male counterparts in them. Together they try and succeed in pinpointing the exact people behind the hoax that made Zam travel to Iraq on what he thought was a business meeting to finance his TV channel in Australia. These sequences are intercut with digital footage of Zam's prolonged official humiliation and sentencing on Iran's state television.

The other major event taking place relates to her personal relation to Zam's family, and to the overt reactions of dissidence performed by both his father (in Iran) and eldest daughter (in France). The latter event is linked to the global protests over the assault on and subsequent demise of Mahsa Amini at the hands of the Iranian security police.

Emblematic images

This film holds very few emblematic images, for natural reasons. There are two short passages of imagery showing a Swedish winter landscape, which offer a welcome narrative pause for the onlooker to collect their thoughts.

As already discussed in relation to her earlier films, cutting up the fabula with this type of emblematic imagery is one of the director's most well-known tropes, and a very thoughtful one. However, this appears only twice in *Son of a Mullah*: after

Figure 6.2 Narrative interval in *Son of a Mullah*. Screenshot by author.

Zam's arrest, and after his death sentence is broadcast on Iranian television. We then get to see her grieving figure standing by the waterside in deep thought.

Discourse versus apparatus

The interplay between discourse and apparatus has evolved significantly since Jane M. Gaines introduced 'political mimesis' and Patricia Zimmermann very cleverly expanded and moved the subject of documentary filmmaking to an 'on-the-ground' pursuit, thus stripping the professional documentarist of their unique privilege to film a certain event. In representing Persson Sarvestani's most complex documentary production to date, *Son of a Mullah* is in its finished form an excellent representative of Zimmermann's idea of how the *enunciator* can use their technical apparatus as a *membrane* to create or contribute a political discourse that expands the media landscape, both formally and discursively.

The role played by so-called on-the-ground footage is a key to its success. According to Zimmermann, in these cases, 'the filmmaking apparatus is alongside the subject, rather than outside it as an observer or chronicler' (Zimmermann 1999: 94). Jihoon Kim characterises the concept as 'a mode of documentary film production that portrays people occupying and struggling on and for [the same] social spaces [as those they document]' (Kim 2022: 201). Since Zimmermann published her work in the late 1990s, mobile phone recordings have become equal to and the most obvious contemporary recording machine for 'on-the-ground' filmmaking. Consequently, this type of footage now embraces any form of documentary recording device handled by anyone present on site.

The second form of on-the-ground filmmaking in *Son of a Mullah* is less combative and was done by the director herself in different locations around the world. This footage is related to different forms of activity performed by fellow exiled journalists working outside Iran, as well as Zam's family and friends. As we have seen, the level of Persson Sarvestani's interaction with her colleagues varies from being merely observational to equally investigative. The unexpected turn of events in this film shows Persson Sarvestani fully immersed, side by side with other exiled Iranian activists who contribute important parts of the film's narrative. They seem to contribute on equal terms, which indicates the director's openness to complete *authorial divestiture*. In discursive terms it also confirms the generally liquid activism of her current documentary practice.

As for the film's narrative, I have already suggested that being her own camera operator was necessary, given the hazardous circumstances and secret nature of some of the operations she undertook during the filming process. In summing up, the filmic fabric of *Son of a Mullah* basically consists of the two above-mentioned forms of on-the-ground filmmaking, with important contextual additions of archival material presenting the political history of Iran and the Zam family's position in relation to it. There are also short cinema intervals of emblematic documentary images.

To make sense to an international film audience, the discursive content of footage filmed on the ground and remediated needs to be placed within an epistolatory framework. In *Son of a Mullah* there are two different forms of this material, as mentioned earlier. The footage filmed on the ground outside Iran by the director herself primarily concerns the case of Rohollo Zam's life and work as an Iranian dissident in exile. This footage is edited in chronological order and quite easy to follow. Documentary footage filmed inside Iran needs a different form of categorisation before its remediation within a specific narrative framework. Jihoon Kim has provided four different labels:

- witnessing videos;
- documentation videos;
- mobilisation videos;
- political mash-ups.

Among these, he holds the first two forms to be the most common and they often take on the character of activist footage (Kim 2022: 195-196). The footage remediated by Persson Sarvestani in *Son of a Mullah* also best fits the labels of 'witness' and 'documentation' videos as they confirm and make important contributions to the topic of her own film, which is unlawful capital punishment, corruption and money laundering.

Conclusion to Part Three

To be clear, when I set out writing this book, the two films presented in this section had not yet been made. As they stand today, they make a pivotal contribution to my effort to reflect Persson Sarvestani's striking ability to hone her documentary practice to current needs in order to spread the word about pertinent political topics. At this point in time, the early 2020s, she decided to follow two exiled Iranian journalists in their daily work to unveil the wrongdoings of the current regime. In the first instance, she presents her inscribed Self as a discursively rather weak sidekick to Masih Alinejad in *Be My Voice*. In the next documentary, *Son of a Mullah*, she becomes more and more immersed in the construction of the film's narrative with time. Towards the end, she is seemingly a full member of the research unit charting the illicit circumstances leading up to Rohollo Zam's execution, as well as its consequences (which includes the footage of Mr Zam Sr renouncing his clerical appointment as mullah). The hands-on documentary mode she opted for is the traditional expository mode whereby she stays close to her documentary subjects during shorter or longer periods of time. From a precursory point of view, it may seem that this operational mode simply requires her to retrace her directorial steps and become an embedded film journalist again. The difference is that she is herself fully inscribed in the narrative both visually and as the finished film product's enunciator. The personal camera thus makes way for both films to retain their label as essay films.

Another reason for my endorsement of this particular ontological framework is the interstitial *vernacular* documentary footage which forms an integral part of the filmic fabric and which Persson Sarvestani brings forth in her editing procedure. I have discussed them in the above sections of the films' different documentary strategies. To sum up, both films presented in this section confirm Jihoon Kim's assertion that 'the camera as "membrane" is no longer a privileged tool for activists or professional filmmakers' (Kim 2022: 201). I hold that by acknowledging this general development within documentary film practice, Persson Sarvestani admits professional documentary filmmakers' dependency on footage filmed by private citizens. It is not only needed to tell the 'whole' story but also because it reflects the situation 'on the ground'. Citizens' witnessing videos have become an ever more important source for documentary filmmakers' work on contemporary issues, and Persson Sarvestani does just the right thing when she edits her films so that they clearly show their contributions on secondary screens – as films in the film, as it were. The multitude of these video clips thus serve the double purpose of both claiming the real and reflecting the widespread nature of a certain action. It would seem that the overall composition of the filmic fabric in *Be My Voice* and *Son of a Mullah* confirms the extent to which the contemporary documentary apparatus depends on *expanded* media to deliver its message. As a result, the inclusion of this type of citizens' witnessing footage can only lead to the further divestment of the director's authorial agency.

Summing up

My study of Nahid Persson Sarvestani's documentaries on Iranian subject matter clearly reflects the necessity to stretch the scholarly definition of documentary filmmaking within the field today. She has covered the subject matter over 20 years with interruptions that have served my critical approach well in that they easily reflect that documentary modes of social and political communication have indeed multiplied and expanded over the years. My study also indicates the degree to which the director has tapped into new modes of documenting for her own, her documentary subjects' and the audiences' benefit. And yet, she has opted to continue 'talking nearby' her subject matter, given its volatile content and varying degree of awareness making depending on who the onlooker is. Further explicating Trinh T. Minh-ha's, by now very famous, statement about the filmmaker's decision to talk *nearby* instead of talking *about*, it acknowledges a speaking that reflects on itself and can come very close to the subject without ultimately seizing or claiming it (Trinh 1999: 209 ff).

What I find interesting about Trinh's statement is that it has affected Persson Sarvestani's documentary practice in so many ways. In terms of the films' narratives, relativism has made it common knowledge that there is no such thing as the complete and final truth. The director thus confesses to the limitation of only being able to speak nearby, without complete knowledge of all facts that affect a certain situation. Opting for this approach, the director also indirectly admits that there is a persistent gap between her and her documentary subjects, regardless of geographical position. I hold that Persson Sarvestani, in acknowledging the existence of this gap and the space of representation it leaves open, has made allowances for different forms of a liquid, divested authorship to come into play, as with the making of *My Stolen Revolution* in 2013. In doing so, the director indirectly acknowledges the effect of different levels of the participatory media culture, which has evolved rapidly and spread online since the early 2010s. She also indicates her awareness and dependence on this media output for her later works.

To clarify my conclusions regarding Nahid Persson Sarvestani's impressive trajectory as a documentary filmmaker on Iranian subject matter, I shall revisit the defining characteristics of her practice, departing from the three main topics mentioned in the book's Introduction. In short, they were listed as the progression of her applied documentary modes, the documentary strategies employed to address and narrativise especially women's experience of the post-revolutionary situation in Iran and, finally, her documentary apparatus in relation to the development of online documentary media.

Persson Sarvestani's applied documentary modes

The director's very first attempt to bridge Iranian subject matter in a documentary mode resulted in *My Mother, A Persian Princess* in the late 1990s. It was commissioned by Swedish Television as an instalment of the TV show *Mosaik*, and never had a theatrical screening. In my view, *My Mother, A Persian Princess* is framed within the traditional set-up of reportage for television. Interacting with a young woman searching for her biological mother in Iran, Persson Sarvestani is fully inscribed in the narrative as this woman's guide and translator. This means that her Self is not performed in the manner required when making documentaries in the essay film mode, but is rather consistent with the requirements of the envisioned TV format.

Persson Sarvestani followed up with two further documentaries on Iranian subject matter in the early 2000s: *Prostitution Behind the Veil* (2004) and *Four Wives, One Man* (2007). They differ from *My Mother* . . . in that they reflect her own choice of topic and are consequently more openly political. Opting for an expository mode allows the director to speak nearby her documentary subjects in a manner which undoubtedly makes the onlooker aware of Fariba's and Mina's precarious social and emotional situation in *Prostitution Behind the Veil*. The image content is closely reflected in the voice-over, and the spectator remains fully immersed in the Iranian subject matter throughout both films. Rather than just being a formal component of the expository mode, the absence of 'behind the scenes' imagery is important to communicate the seriousness of both films' narratives to the audience. The fullness of Persson Sarvestani's choice of documentary mode is also easily detected if compared to Mahnaz Afzali's film *The Ladies' Room*, which was made at about the same time as *Prostitution Behind the Veil*. Afzali theoretically uses a similar documentary approach, but in her film the women visiting the public bathroom are exposed to her intrusive camera in a manner predicating on outright confrontation and condescendence on the director's part. As a result, the film presents the women not as victims but as offenders.

An important common denominator in Persson Sarvestani's first three films is that they are filmed in situ, in Iran. Access to the locale was critical when it came to the choice of subject matter for her first two feature-length documentaries.

I consequently hold that being denied further entry to Iran as from 2006, during the production of *Four Wives, One Man*, may have been perceived as a pivotal blow to her career as a professional documentarist at the time. In hindsight we see, however, that being denied access to this particular documentary subject matter invited Persson Sarvestani to investigate new types of authorship, as well as hitherto uncharted documentary modes.

Having already experienced filmmaking in the first person, opting to make further use of self-inscription probably seemed like the most natural way to proceed. Besides the effect on her documentary apparatus, it also meant that Persson Sarvestani was offered an opportunity to look further into her own family history, and especially her brother Rostam's premature death in the early days of post-revolutionary Iran. At this point, not having access to Iranian territory also prompted a new discursive approach along the lines of Trinh T. Min-ha's notion of 'speaking nearby' as I discussed above.

Starting from *The Queen and I*, Persson Sarvestani around 2010 achieves a more personal manner of documentary practice using first-person filmmaking. Unlike the two previous documentaries, this film is a portrait film based on the filmmaker's personal meetings with Farah Pahlavi. The mere audacity of the film's topic – not to mention the inscription of herself in the same frame with an unattainable Iranian royal person – must have stunned Iranians worldwide, seeing as the Shah and his family were untouchable, even godlike, to ordinary Iranians, including Persson Sarvestani's own family. And certainly, the director's main objective with the film failed, in that the former queen did not accept the political challenge the director wanted to confront her with. It could be said that Persson Sarvestani opted for a new approach by befriending her enemy and completely reconfiguring the film's *sujet*. She confesses in her memoir that '[a]s a filmmaker I now realized the potential of the subject matter; Farah as the surviving symbol of a regime which had been extremely elevated and deeply hated' (Persson Sarvestani 2011: 291–292, my translation). As a result, *The Queen and I* is in many ways a flawed documentary film, although many exiled Iranians say it is her best work. The cause of my dismay is grounded in the fact that the discourse of regret delivered in the voice-over narrative stands in such blatant contrast to the hearty, almost intimate visuals that make up the filmic fabric. Seeing the director having such a nice time with Farah Pahlavi in tandem with the film's voice-over continuously sharing her distress around this 'surrender' with the spectator is most unnerving in the end.

Positioning the film as a formal experiment of double portraiture, *The Queen and I* was thus robbed of its interpellative momentum in responding to the film's original *objectif*. The question is therefore whether stepping into the Queen's aura was worth it from a directorial point of view. It was certainly worth it in terms of popular reception because, according to Rascaroli, '[o]ne cannot stress enough the importance of the body in the self-portrait' (Rascaroli 2009: 185–186), exemplified as 'the historicised body of [a former highly elevated queen]; as a filmic body – a flickering [and] intensely iconic and desirable image' (Rascaroli 2009: 186–187).

From a sociopolitical standpoint, Trinh T. Minh-ha has stated:

> To understand the political dimension of our personal lives, we constantly have to look into the ways we position ourselves and the different context in which we operate. Thanks to the awareness of our positionality in everything we do, our activities are no longer compartmentalized as if they could be sufficient in themselves, and what is thought to be personal can no longer be limited to the individual and the singular. (Trinh 1999: 46)

In terms of Persson Sarvestani's progress within the domain of documentary authorship, I hold that the director, in acknowledging the existence of this gap in the body politic, and the space of representation it leaves open in *The Queen and I*, invited a new form of liquid, divested authorship to come into play. It comes to clear fruition in her following, in my view most unravelling, documentary, *My Stolen Revolution* from 2013. Applying a meta perspective, it could be said that the director, by embracing such authorial fluidity, indirectly acknowledges the effect of different levels of participatory media culture on documentary practice since the early 2010s. She also indicates her awareness and acceptance of this online media output in relation to her own working conditions.

The director's professional divestment of her authorship finds its form in *My Stolen Revolution*, which is a thematic study of Iranian women's incarceration in their home country for their political beliefs during the 1980s and '90s. Inviting a total of five other women to contribute their history to the film's thematic narrative allowed for a polyvocal film fabric that unreservedly enriched and certified its epistemological premise. The slightly varying time frames of the women's experiences allowed Persson Sarvestani to add yet other diegetic as well as extra-diegetic diachronic dimensions to the finished film. In the recording process, she for instance opted for a dual set-up of the women's performance whereby she took their witness statements individually in their homes before she brought them all together for a continued round-table discussion about their memories and experiences in a neutral location. The time lapse between the two events gave the women time to think and reflect on memories some of them had tried very hard to internalise, or even forget.

Featured as an extension of but still fully relevant to the main narrative storyline, the director additionally persuaded these brave women to perform a silent pantomime. This act adds yet another diachronic layer to the film's fabric by indicating both personal experiences gone by in terms of costume while at the same time performing in a manner which calls for further political action on a symbolic level.

Regarding Persson Sarvestani's own contribution to the film's narrative, I suggest that her lack of personal experience of political incarceration and torture brings Trinh's notion of speaking nearby to its highest potential. Persson Sarvestani rightfully includes footage that positions her as the film's absolute enunciator and mastermind, and yet the onlooker is made fully aware of the fact that the director herself is *not close enough* to her subject matter to discuss it in detail. Opting for a divested form of authorship was thus a necessary means if she wanted to maintain the film's topic and raise cinema audiences' awareness about this particular political situation.

Persson Sarvestani's liquid position as director, enunciator and subject through the different set-ups in her essay films was a result of its narrative. I additionally argue that *My Stolen Revolution* shows that the notion of divested authorship in tandem with third-wave feminism can be used to move Rascaroli's original theory on essay film forward, underpinned by Persson Sarvestani's experimental approach to its tenets.

The overall discursive aim of this book is to establish the nature of Persson Sarvestani's authorship as a contemporary, deeply political first-person documentarist. I claim that she has used a selection of documentary strategies to form her work, yet she never wavered in her position as the films' enunciator despite the influence and diffusion caused by citizens' contending online documentary media offerings. This development is confirmed by her reversion to a more traditional form of expository documentary mode in her two latest documentaries, *Be My Voice* and *Son of a Mullah*.

Be My Voice is a traditional documentary portrait film, entirely devoted to Masih Alinejad's work as an oppositional Iranian TV journalist working in exile in the United States. Except for short excerpts of archival film, this film reflects the massive amount of online documentary media that Alinejad relies on to initiate, produce and broadcast political counter-narratives via satellite. Persson Sarvestani joins her effort through different acts of remediation, which again instils her work with a fluid authorship which can be identified as both political and collective in nature. *Be My Voice*, however, does not present a political narrative based on interviews with Alinejad, and therefore relies on messages conveyed through different connotations of visual character. Hence, I centred my discussion of its discursive remits on the film's politically framed body politic based on ideas and theories offered by Patricia Zimmermann and Jacky Stacey. I showed that their concepts from the late 1990s are indeed applicable to scholarly discussions of the physical nature of political discourse at any time, everywhere around the globe.

Son of a Mullah was intellectually conceptualised at the time of the production of *Be My Voice*. In fact, they partly overlap with each other. The arrest and jailing of Rohollo Zam forced Persson Sarvestani to put her documentary on him on hold. The completed film tells the story of his life and journalistic effort to shed light on the Iranian regime while living in exile in France. In *Son of a Mullah* the director reverts to an expository documentary mode partly predicated on her own investigative efforts together with a team of other Iranian journalists. The film fabric is hence completely chronological, and more than ever points to the joint authorial effort contributing to its content. From a directorial point of view, this suggestion begs the question of the consequences of authorial divestiture. It seems to me that Persson Sarvestani has by now completely left the idea of an authorship based on the Romantic tradition behind in favour of the professional clout achieved though collective authorship.

According to Trinh and her concept of the body politic, this seems to be a foregone professional development given the topic at hand:

> The body does not simply point to an individual terrain; it is the site where the individual and society meet. And it is by working on the relationship that the tension between the personal and the political is maintained and kept alive in writing. (Trinh 1999: 46)

Discursively, *Son of a Mullah* chronicles a very fast-paced and complicated narrative, placing high demands on the spectator. Persson Sarvestani provides necessary intellectual breaks through emblematic imagery at intervals throughout the film. These visual intervals offer the onlooker time to comprehend the information set forth in the narrative.

Non-diegetic imagery as a documentary strategy

Persson Sarvestani's documentary film practice has taken unexpected turns over the years, and my study in this book strongly suggests that the political and feminist hallmarks that characterise it, as well as the terms of production that inform it, have been subject to continuous modification over the past 30 years.

Regardless of formal changes to the main narrative discourse, the use of aesthetic and/or self-reflexive tropes has remained a constant element in one form or another in Persson Sarvestani's films on Iranian subject matter. These aesthetic/self-reflexive tropes have nothing in common with iconicity in that they do not refer to previously well-known imagery that has risen to fame in the eyes of the public through repeated publication. Instead, in Persson Sarvestani's films, this imagery, often labelled as 'pillow shots', has a certain affinity with those abstract images first seen in East Asian fictional films by, for instance, Yazujiro Ozu or Kon Ichikawa. For the most part, this is non-consequential footage, which I see as generally representing a narrative interval making room for intellectual contemplation. The question is what iconographical content this footage iterates, and what effect such non-diegetic imagery has had on the discursive level and overall political narrative in Persson Sarvestani's documentaries.

Prostitution Behind the Veil

Looking at her early films, *Prostitution Behind the Veil* (2004) and *Four Wives, One Man* (2007), they show a clearly objective and consistent relationship between image, narrative and voice-over commentaries. The director alludes to the women's absolute vulnerability by framing them in deep shadows, as for instance when we see Farina standing by the roadside with her son, in the dusk, waiting for a john to pick them up in his car. These shadows increase the sense of their isolation from ordinary society, but – and this is important here – the footage still taps fully into the film's overall narrative about heroin addiction and prostitution, both constituting felonies in their country. These women are outcasts, and the director draws our attention to their precarious living conditions by framing them either in isolation in their temporary living quarters or in the darkness of night. The clear emphasis on objective information and enlightenment about their delicate situation prevents the director from using non-diegetic imagery in *Prostitution Behind the Veil*.

Four Wives, One Man

This film was made in traditional cinema verité style, again with minimal interference from the director. Mainly because of its openly investigating purpose into an emotionally very complicated situation, the film is dominated by interviews and remediated in a talking-heads format. The voice-over narrative is inconsequential and sparse.

Realising that the film's topic would be very demanding on a Western audience, the director halts the narrative by inserting ethnographically framed emblematic imagery of the beautiful but harsh Iranian countryside where the family lives. Yet another interval is created through imagery of the entire family going on a madcap picnic in an old bus, assisted by footage of the women at the loom weaving or knotting carpets. The lightness and beauty of this ethnographic imagery admittedly brings a certain paucity to the narrative, and is of limited importance for the film's overall very dramatic discourse about social and emotional stigma.

The Queen and I

From *The Queen and I* (2008) onwards, Persson Sarvestani's documentaries on Iranian subject matter include emblematic imagery. The overall narrative of this film fits well with the characteristics of 'comparative exilism and diasporism' that are key to Hamid Naficy's notion of accented cinema. Consequently, the discursive role played by different forms of non-diegetic imagery in this film is informed by nostalgia.

Part of its emblematic imagery consists of archival TV footage from Iranian broadcasts presenting the Shah's and Farah Pahlavi's illustrious lives as King and Queen. This footage is now deeply coveted among certain Iranian exiles. What is more interesting and unexpected, however, is Persson Sarvestani's effort to restage that splendour and nostalgia of ancient nobility's picnicking by inserting imagery of the Queen *and herself* picnicking under a parasol on the lawn in front of the former's American mansion. Seemingly unproblematic on the surface because of its vernacular familiarity in visual culture, the *actual* appearance of a film director from a very modest background picnicking in the company of Iran's former queen is an anomaly of gigantic proportions.

My Stolen Revolution

This documentary revolves around a group of exiled Iranian women's experience of being jailed for their political acts of resistance in Tehran in the early 1980s. It contains yet another form of non-diegetic imagery which is more to do with the different political and discursive challenges that emerged during the film's production. Persson Sarvestani admits to her worries and doubts in her voice-over comments, but also by inserting a different type of imagery in the film's fabric.

In these short passages we see her standing in deep thought by the waterside outside her studio in Sweden. She has her back turned towards the camera and is staring into thin air, seemingly oblivious of the beautiful scenery around her. I have elsewhere in this book referred to this set-up as showing the director in a thinking pose, self-reflexively reasserting her position as the film's enunciator. Intentionally or not, these images also offer an intellectual pause by pulling the spectator away from the film's main topic by presenting them with a beautiful view.

To further sharpen the film's discursive premise in relation to current events at the time, the director asked the women to perform a silent pantomime in addition to their testimonies. In these scenes, the women appear one by one quietly before the camera, dressed in the atonement outfit used to brainwash them into becoming faithful Muslims during their time of incarceration.

In the pantomime, the women play out the reverse story by first standing still, completely covered and wearing eye masks, until they suddenly and impatiently remove their veils with a grand gesture and voluptuously ruffle their hair. These scenes are identical, and each performance is less than two minutes long. They at first come across as non-diegetic, but on reflection, it is difficult not to see them as an expression of covert political activism.

Be My Voice

Almost ten years later, in 2021, Persson Sarvestani released *Be My Voice* addressing contemporary female subjectivity inside Iran. The narrative reflects the moment when young Iranian women had begun officially discarding their veils on camera and posting the footage on social media. Already at the beginning of the film, we see compiled versions of the silent pantomime from *My Stolen Revolution* being performed by Iranian women from all social strata. At this point during the production of the film, in 2020, the act had been initiated by Masih Alinejad as an internet-driven act of activism under the hashtag 'White Wednesday'. This transition of the original act, and its rebooted appearance on the internet, signals 'a use of the documentary image elevated to the status of icon by virtue of its connection to an original event' (Gaines 1999: 96). Alinejad and her campaigns on Instagram to empower Iranian women's resistance to the regime prompted Nahid Persson Sarvestani to make *Be My Voice*.

What I have asked is whether the *reiteration* of the initial act, the new versions of the act itself, as well as its exhibition in compiled form by first Alinejad in her digital news programme *Tablet* and then by Persson Sarvestani in *Be My Voice*, gives reason to reconsider its discursive meaning. Does the compilation of the many, but identical, iterations of this act, whether still or moving, represent a more political form of emblematic imagery? In terms of production, there are silent performances by women filming themselves discarding their veils. There are also films of women discarding them, even burning them, in front of large crowds, being filmed by others. If they can indeed be seen as representing a more political form of emblematic imagery, the onlooker comes to this conclusion without any voiced opinions by either Persson Sarvestani or Alinejad. It means that the remediation itself is enough to make the connection between the strong implications surrounding the veil, and politics, and communicates the message. The medium is the message.

I also ask whether the pronounced polyvocal character of the film's discourse accounts for the lack of self-reflexive imagery implicating the director as the film's one and only enunciator in *Be My Voice*. Persson Sarvestani's role as the film's director is continuously pared down to the advantage of Alinejad. There is only footage of her working and carrying out household chores at home in Sweden, maintaining contact with Alinejad and being continuously observant of the digital feed on her devices in relation to Iranian affairs. From the spectator's perspective, these short passages, however, again offer a certain discursive paucity by reflecting attempts at 'normality'.

Son of a Mullah

In Nahid Persson Sarvestani's latest documentary, *Son of a Mullah* (2023), she assists other investigating journalists in their attempts to clarify the circumstances leading to Zam's demise. The actual dangers involved in their ongoing, multivocal activism and agency requires the director to stop and think carefully about her proceedings and how to navigate through them. These situations of deep reflection on her part are again illustrated with the same type of self-reflexive imagery that can be seen in *My Stolen Revolution*, supplemented by expository documentary footage of herself conducting research on her computer and following the official humiliation of Rohollo Zam in different programmes on Iranian television.

My scholarly purpose with this material has been to theoretically unpick what effect non-diegetic imagery has had on the discursive level and overall political narrative in Persson Sarvestani's films since the early twenty-first century. I have found that the variation of this imagery in the director's documentary practice defies one single definition. Generally speaking, the non-diegetic imagery in her early documentaries does not have a definite bearing on the film's overall narrative discourse and film fabric, as seen in *Four Wives, One Man* or *The Queen and I*. Informed by wordless nostalgia, this type of emblematic imagery seems to additionally instil a pause by temporarily simply breaking off the film's main narrative. The onlooker gets a few seconds to get their head around what is really going on, very much in the same manner as the director seems to be doing.

As her films became more discursively complicated, the ethnographic imagery was replaced by self-reflexive imagery, to reinstate Persson Sarvestani as its strong enunciator. By doing so, she seems to somehow have taken back control and asserted her authorial right to the films' overall *sujet* regardless of their multivocal narratives. As for the politically emblematic characteristics of certain digital imagery, it is my contention that it reflects Persson Sarvestani's willingness to customise her documentary practice in relation to society's changing patterns of communication.

Persson Sarvestani's documentary apparatus in relation to the development of online documentary media

Putting Persson Sarvestani's film into perspective, there is little doubt that her almost decade-long absence from political documentary-making, forced Nahid Persson Sarvestani to take yet another step away from its traditional conditions and modes of production in 2020. Citing Angela J. Aguayo, the documentary impulse has become 'a way of life and articulation of political information and [its] democratic exchange constitute new patterns of public communication' (Aguayo 2019: 227).

Hence, the director's practice again changed considerably compared to her films from previous decades. And yet, *Be My Voice* and *Son of a Mullah* are completely distinct from one another, despite having at times existed as 'twin projects' on the director's table.

According to Jihoon Kim, one of the key changes in the hybrid docmedia ecosystem relates to the collection, distribution and consumption of visible evidence, both as separate entities making up a documentary's lifespan and as a whole. Regarding the collection of material, she compares the production processes defining traditional activist film and video-making as well as the political documentary to contemporary online activist documentary practice. Most of the former productions are intended for exhibition in cinema theatres and the like, whereas online documentaries are distributed digitally, resulting in much higher viewing numbers as they are consumed in many different media formats and alternative outlets. Providing extensive examples from, for example, the unrest in Hong Kong around 2020 and the Arab Spring (2010–2013), Kim shows that the transmedia strategies embraced by online activist documentaries are much more effective when it comes to creating political awareness and mobilisation also among ordinary citizens. What Persson Sarvestani does is to find ways to combine traditional and digital forms of documentary footage in her practice. A necessary prerequisite for this development of her documentary practice is her lack of concern over the fact that the mobile phone has now become the most common recording device, and that it is often placed in the hands of citizens rather than a professional documentarist. This transition of the technical machinery was perhaps the first sign of an expanded, and hence more global, docmedia landscape (and not for the first time, considering the changes in production modes in documentary filmmaking brought about by, for example, portable filming equipment in the 1950s).

When it comes to the effects of this recording transition on the overall conditions of production, it entails the abandon of *authorial control* over both available footage and the entire scene of events being documented when making a film. The effect of this expansion in original media resources on a professional documentary filmmaker like Nahid Persson Sarvestani – who has emerged as both willing to use and depending on remediated footage shot by others in her latest works – is that her authorial control has been repositioned and moved forward to the editing process. But that is not all. Persson Sarvestani has simultaneously demonstrated her understanding and willingness to embrace the authorial divestiture that is a necessary result of such an expanded docmedia ecosystem.

Applicable mainly to her latest films, *Be My Voice* comes across as a more clear-cut case of authorial divestiture in that it focuses on a documentary subject whose daily routines and professional agenda is traditionally rather predictable. Because she is herself fully inscribed in the footage, we can see that the director's interaction with Masih Alinejad is primarily observational and/ or expository. Persson Sarvestani does not have an investigative agenda of her own to contribute to the film's narrative, which stands in stark contrast to the evolving discourse of *Son of a Mullah*. The filmic fabric of the latter was always impossible to foresee, mainly because it involved several journalists', at times separate, investigations.

A joint characteristic in both films is the prolific use of – and dependence on – on-the-ground footage by private citizens. This material had sometimes been distributed on the internet before it was either trawled or redistributed directly to Alinejad and her colleagues, as evidence of ongoing or recently occurred events. It is then again remediated and reframed in Persson Sarvestani's two films. This type of footage in particular enhances the degree of spectator immersion through political mimesis, especially those clips where Iranian women discard their veils.

I have previously discussed Persson Sarvestani's documentary practice in relation to Jane M. Gaines' concept of 'political mimesis.' The notion is based on Sergei Eisenstein's theories on how cinema can effect social change, based on the suggestion that 'the bodily senses lead the spectator, whose involvement is not strictly intellectual – politics is not exclusively a matter of the head but can also be a matter of the heart' (Gaines 1999: 88). Since political mimesis is based on an aesthetic of similarity, the film can succeed in establishing 'a continuity between the world of the screen and the world of the audience' if it touches and motivates the onlooker on an emotional level (Gaines 1999: 92).

Dispersing authorial control shows, it seems to me, that the expanded docmedia landscape we now see consequently and fundamentally strengthens the filmmaker's role as *enunciator*. Compared to online activist footage, the enunciator of traditional documentary film products for theatrical exhibition has an established platform to project from. The exhibited film product thus revolves around the enunciator's idea on its core topic and filmic presentation, and the final cut entails, in particular, how it is framed discursively to obtain and secure 'political mimesis'.

This hybrid docmedia ecosystem simultaneously demands as much as invites new approaches to the dissemination of visible evidence. A pertinent example of this development would be the fact that Persson Sarvestani allows the political discourse in *Be My Voice* to take a slightly new direction towards the end of the film, thus confirming her willingness to engage with documentary material that inherently reflects a more disparate social awareness.

In such an expanded media landscape, a certain conceptual hybridity is central to any documentary discourse dealing with matters pertaining to inter/national political activism. *Be My Voice* clearly shows that in relation to documentary production, conceptual hybridity may involve creating a montage of Persson Sarvestani's objectively shot footage with different forms of individually produced activist footage to present a coherent product to the onlooker. When such a media assemblage is remediated within someone else's documentary narrative, the production mode of witness or documentation videos, for instance, may take on a secondary meaning, to the advantage of their political content. The pronounced original character of online documentary media activism is thus downplayed to the benefit of the overriding discourse related to Masih Alinejad's work in a film such as *Be My Voice*. This transition occurs, for instance, when Alinejad remediates the citizen-camera-witnessing videos in compiled form on her own social media channels, or in her TV programme, or when they contribute to the film fabric of *Be My Voice*. Such secondary emissions of witness or documentation videos reflect their transition into 'mobilization videos', Jihoon Kim's notion defining short-form documentaries that 'urge viewers to join the protest in the streets, [or] to engage discussion on its related issues' (Kim 2022: 196). Appearing as a digital form of Jane M. Gaines' notion of 'political mimesis', one of the main obstacles for its exhibition success that Gaines foresaw at the time was its 'loose montage structure [which] is perhaps less aesthetically potent than the featured documentary footage, and it is as though the video makers are deferring [to] the power of the images themselves' (Gaines 1999: 96). Now, 25 years later, the appearance of blurry and shaky images are no longer 'awkward' features in documentary films. They are not even considered to be an aesthetic drawback harming the production's main topic, but a natural and necessary component of its realist nature. The main reason for documentary aesthetics' reduced importance on the discursive level is, of course, our increased familiarity with witness and documentation footage registered via citizens' handheld mobile phones.

Returning to the terms of their documentary production, Kari Andén-Papadopoulos has coined the term 'citizen-camera-witnessing' for this type of action by bystanders, describing it as 'ritualized employment of mobile camera as a personal witnessing device to provide a public record of embodied actions of political dissent for the purpose of persuasion' (Andén-Papadopoulos 2014: 756). Kim elaborates on Papadopoulos' definition of the recording as an act of self-inscription at the event by suggesting that providing such visible evidence of turbulence and abuse can no longer be seen as merely self-referential or inscribing their own embodied experience through the act of filming. According to Kim, such acts additionally 'attest to the filming citizen's affective and corporeal immersion in the protest', which must be understood as their consenting to the event (Kim 2022: 198). The many videos showing Iranian women unveiling themselves form an example of such bystander immersion and attest to Gaines' hypothesis on the emotive power of 'political mimesis'.

Beyond its role as visible evidence, this footage was technically produced with a mobile camera, which indicates the extent to which digital techniques constitute an important part of the political apparatus informing the remediation of, for instance, violations of human rights in different parts of the world today. Online documentary activism via social media has now taken over as an integral part – perhaps even the most essential technical dissemination device – of the Iranian countermovement toady. Persson Sarvestani's documentary practice in her two latest films fully embraces this development through its repeated remediation of different forms of visible evidence, such as that which Alinejad shows her on her handheld devices.

What role do they play when Persson Sarvestani remediates them in her own films? I suggest that opting for a documentary method based on remediation results in a trickling-down effect which renders Persson Sarvestani and her film practice as politically activistic as Alinejad's or any other of the filmmaker's colleagues' first-hand interventions. The resulting documentary product in Persson Sarvestani's case is, however, meant for a completely different – but equally important – audience. Regardless of form, any exhibited visible evidence thus ultimately depends on identification with the audiences for its success.

Finally, I suggest that Persson Sarvestani's transition from the auteurism of a traditional documentary practice to one that is more liquid is the most formally tangible result of Persson Sarvestani being forced to find her subject matter outside Iran. This porous mode of documentary practice furthermore aligns well with the essay film format's openness and resistance 'to crystalize into a genre' embraced by the director over the past decades (Rascaroli 2009: 39).

As a result, the inclusion of this type of citizens' witnessing footage can only lead to the director's authorial agency being further divested. Nahid Persson Sarvestani's career as a documentary filmmaker thus stands in stark contrast to Majed Naesi's documentary effort in *Inside the Iranian Uprising*, for instance. Even though the latter is partly composed of footage similar to that which we see in *Be My Voice* especially, Naesi's film hinges discursively only on reference to and comment about external documentary footage. I suggest that this material's ontological as well as discursive limits has a distancing effect on the documentary mode used to present it, which is traditionally expository.

Persson Sarvestani's personal investment in her professional practice thus makes a considerable difference when it comes to the discursive quality and ensuing consciousness-raising affordances regarding political subject matter in contemporary documentary filmmaking. I contend that it would not have been possible to embrace this new direction within her profession had she not also accepted the discursive affordances made available through authorial divestiture. Refuting the Romantic idea of singlehanded authorship indeed became a practical necessity when she could no longer record her documentary footage in situ. I hold that even if she had been able to do so, the evolution of online documentary activism had still encouraged her to discursively abandon the traditional way of making politically relevant documentaries. The director's openminded and courageous approach to her work has thus moved contemporary documentary filmmaking in a distinctly new, less auteur-driven direction. This new wave of liquid authorship in documentary filmmaking now guarantees that the truth will always come out.

References

Adra, Najwa. 2009. 'Four Wives – One Man'. *Visual Anthropology Review* 25(1): 103–105.
Aguayo, Angela J. 2019. *Documentary Resistance: Social Change and Participatory Media*. New York: Oxford University Press.
Ahmadi, Tania. 2023. '"Woman, Life, Freedom" – a Feminist Revolution Against Police Atrocity'. *Jump Cut: A Review of Contemporary Media* 62, Winter 2023–24.
Ahmed, Leila. 2003. 'The Discourse of the Veil'. In *Veiling, Representation and Contemporary Art*, edited by David A. Bailey and Gilane Tawadros. London: Institute of International Visual Arts. 40–55.
Alter, Nora M., and Timothy Corrigan (eds). 2017. *Essays on the Essay Film*. New York: Columbia University Press.
Andén-Papadopoulos, Kari. 2014. 'Citizen Camera-Witnessing: Embodied Political Dissent in the Age of "Mediated Mass Self-communication"'. *New Media & Society* 16(5): 753–769.
Bauman, Zygmunt. 2000. *Liquid Modernity*. Cambridge: Polity Press.
Boussoualim, Malika. 2021. 'Veiling Between Denigration and Glorification in Algeria'. *Sexuality & Culture* 25(4): 1290–1307. https://doi.org/10.1007/s12119-021-09825-w
Bruzzi, Stella. 2000. *New Documentary: A Critical Introduction*. London: Routledge.
Buckland, Warren (ed.). 1995. *The Film Spectator: From Sign to Mind*. Amsterdam: Amsterdam University Press.
Burton, Julianne. 1990. *The Social Documentary in Latin America*. Pittsburgh: University of Pittsburgh Press.
Chadwick, Andrew. 2017. *The Hybrid Media System: Politics and Power* (2nd edn). New York: Oxford University Press.
Doane, Mary Ann. 2003. 'The Close-up: Scale and Detail in the Cinema'. *Differences: A Journal of Feminist Cultural Studies* 14: 89–111.

Fish, Laura. 2020. 'Remixing Vulgarity: Reinterpreting the Legacy of Popular Iranian Cinema'. *The Velvet Light Trap* 85: 533–564.
Fontini, Pinar. 2022. 'Her Resistance Is Many: The Accented Filmmaking Practice of Mizgin Müjde Arslan'. *Feminist Media Studies*. https://doi.org/10.1080/14680777.2022.2048046
Gaines, Jane M. 1999. 'Political Mimesis'. In *Collecting Visible Evidence*, edited by Jane M. Gaines and Michael Renov. Minneapolis, MN and London: University of Minnesota Press. 84–102.
Gaines, Jane M., and Michael Renov (eds). 1999. *Collecting Visible Evidence*. Minneapolis, MN and London: University of Minnesota Press.
Johnston, Claire. 1973. 'Women's Cinema as Counter Cinema'. In *Notes on Women's Cinema*, edited by Claire Johnston. London: Society for Education in Film and Television. Reprinted in Bill Nichols, ed. 1979. *Movies and Methods*. Berkeley, CA: University of California Press.
Kaplan, E. A. 1997. *Looking for the Other: Feminism, Film and the Imperial Gaze*. London: Routledge.
Kim, Jihoon. 2022. *Documentary's Expanded Fields*. Oxford: Oxford University Press.
Kuhn, Annette. 2002 [1995]. *Family Secrets: Acts of Memory and Imagination*. London: Verso.
LaRocca, David (ed.). 2023. *Metacinema: The Form and Content of Filmic Reference and Reflexivity*. Oxford: Oxford University Press.
Lebow, Alisa (ed.). 2012. *The Cinema of Me: The Self and Subjectivity in First Person Documentary*. London and New York: Wallflower Press.
Lebow, Alisa S. 2008. *First Person Jewish*. Minneapolis, MN and London: University of Minnesota Press.
Lesage, Julia. 1990. 'Women Make Media: Three Modes of Production'. In *The Social Documentary in Latin America*, edited by Julianne Burton. Pittsburgh, PA: University of Pittsburgh Press. 315–347.
Lesage, Julia. 1978. 'The Political Aesthetics of the Feminist Documentary Film'. *Quarterly Review of Film Studies* 3(4): 507–523.
Merás, Lidia. 2018. 'Profession: Documentarist: Underground Documentary Making in Iran'. In *Female Agency and Documentary Strategies: Subjectivities, Identity, and Activism*, edited by Boel Ulfsdotter and Anna Backman Rogers. Edinburgh: Edinburgh University Press. 170–183.
Metz, Christian. 1995. 'The Impersonal Enunciation, or the Site of Film: In the Margin of Recent Works on Enunciation in Cinema'. In *The Film Spectator: From Sign to Mind*, edited by Warren Buckland. Amsterdam: Amsterdam University Press. 140–163.
Mina, An Xiao. 2019. *Memes to Movements: How the World's Most Viral Media Is Changing Social Protest and Power*. Boston, MA: Beacon Press.

Molony, Barbara, and Jennifer Nelson (eds). 2017. *Women's Activism and 'Second Wave' Feminism: Transnational Histories*. London and New York: Bloomsbury Academic.

Mulvey, Laura. 1975. 'Visual Pleasure and Narrative Cinema'. *Screen* 16(3): 6–18.

Naficy, Hamid. 2001. *An Accented Cinema: Exilic and Diasporic Filmmaking*. Princeton, NJ: Princeton University Press.

Naficy, Hamid. 2003. 'Poetics and Politics of Veil, Voice and Vision in Iranian Post-revolutionary Cinema'. In *Veiling, Representation and Contemporary Art*, edited by David A. Bailey and Gilane Tawadros. London: Institute of International Visual Arts. 138–159.

Nichols, Bill. 1991. *Representing Reality: Issues and Concepts of Documentary*. Bloomington and Indianapolis, IN: Indiana University Press.

Nichols, Bill. 2010. *Introduction to Documentary*, 2nd ed. Bloomington and Indianapolis, IN: Indiana University Press.

Persson Sarvestani, Nahid. 2011. *Alltid I mitt hjärta*. Stockholm: Bladh by Bladh.

Pollock, Griselda. 2007. 'Liquid Modernity and Cultural Analysis'. *Theory, Culture & Society* 24(1): 111–116. https://doi.org/10.1177/0263276407071578

Poudeh, Reza. 2010. 'Women Make Movies: Documentary Film by Iranian Women'. *Iranian Studies* 43(3): 411–417.

Rascaroli, Laura. 2008. 'The Essay Film: Problems, Definitions, Textual Commitments'. *Framework: The Journal of Cinema and Media* 49(2): 24–47.

Rascaroli, Laura. 2009. *The Personal Camera: Subjective Cinema and the Essay Film*. London and New York: Wallflower Press.

Renov, Michael. 2004. *The Subject of Documentary*. Minneapolis, MN and London: University of Minnesota Press.

Sabur, Abdus. 2022. 'Gender, Veiling, and Class: Symbolic Boundaries and Veiling in Bengali Muslim Families'. *Gender & Society* 36(3): 397–421. https://doi.org/10.1177/08912432221089631

Sayad, Cecilia. 2013. *Performing Authorship: Self-inscription and Corporeality in the Cinema*. London: I.B. Tauris.

Shifman, Limor. 2014. *Memes in Digital Culture*. Cambridge, MA and London: MIT Press.

Suner, Asuman. 2007. 'Cinema without Frontiers: Transnational Women's Filmmaking in Iran and Turkey'. In *Transnational Feminism in Film and Media*, edited by Marciniak, Katarzyna, Anikó Imre and Áine O'Healy. London and New York: Palgrave Macmillan. 53–70.

Trinh, T. Minh-Ha. 1999. *Cinema Interval*. London and New York: Routledge.

Ulfsdotter, Boel. 2019. 'Nahid Persson Sarvestani: Female Auteur'. *MAI – Feminism & Visual Culture* 3. https://maifeminism.com/nahid-persson-sarvestani-female-auteur/

Van de Peer, Stefanie. 2018. *Negotiating Dissidence: The Pioneering Women of Arab Documentary*. Edinburgh: Edinburgh University Press.
White, Patricia. 2015. *Women's Cinema, World Cinema: Projecting Contemporary Feminisms*. Durham, NC: Duke University Press.
Yu, Kiki Tianqi. 2019. *'My" Self on Camera: First Person Documentary Practice in an Individualising China*. Edinburgh: Edinburgh University Press.
Yacavone, Daniel. 2023. 'Recursive Reflections: Types, Modes, and Form of Cinematic Reflexibility'. In *Metacinema: The Form and Content of Filmic Reference and Reflexibility*, edited by David LaRocca. Oxford: Oxford University Press. 85–113.
Zimmermann, Patricia R. 2000. *States of Emergency: Documentaries, Wars, Democracies*. Minneapolis, MN and London: University of Minnesota Press.

Filmographies

Digital downloads

Akbari, Mina: www.wiko-berlin.de/fellows/akademisches-jahr/2023/akbari-mina (accessed 22 February 2023)
IMDB: Jean-Luc Godard, filmography www.imdb.com/name/nm0000419/?ref_=fn_al_nm_1 (accessed 18 January 2023)
Iranian Women's Film Festival: https://iranianwomenfilmfestival.eventive.org (accessed 20 February 2023)

Nahid Persson Sarvestani as director

Persson Sarvestani, Nahid. *Anders, Me and His 23 Other Women* (Sweden, 2018)
Persson Sarvestani, Nahid. *Be My Voice* (Sweden, 2021)
Persson Sarvestani, Nahid. *Four Wives, One Man* (Sweden, 2007)
Persson Sarvestani, Nahid. *My Mother, A Persian Princess* (Sweden, 2000)
Persson Sarvestani, Nahid. *My Stolen Revolution* (Sweden, 2013)
Persson Sarvestani, Nahid. *Prostitution Behind the Veil* (Sweden, 2004)
Persson Sarvestani, Nahid. *Queen and I, The* (Sweden, 2008)
Persson Sarvestani, Nahid. *Seventeen Years of Longing* (Sweden, 1997)
Persson Sarvestani, Nahid. *Son of a Mullah.* (Sweden, 2023)

Nahid Persson Sarvestani, TV productions

Mosaik (Swedish Television, 1987–2003)

Other films

Abtahi, Sepideh, Shirin Barghnavard and Mina Keshavarz. *Profession: Documentarist* (Iran, 2014)
Afzali, Mahnaz. *Mother of the Earth* (Iran, 2017)
Afzali, Mahnaz. *The Ladies' Room* (Iran, 2003)
Akbari, Mania. *How Dare You Have Such a Rubbish Wish* (Iran, 2022)
Akbari, Mina. *Formerly Youth Square* (Iran, 2019).
Akbari, Mina. *Women of the Revolution* (work in progress)
Allen, Catherine, Judy Irola and Allie Light. *Self-Health* (USA, 1974)
Arslan, Mizgin Müjde. *A Fatal Dress: Polygamy* (Turkey, 2009)
Bani-Etemad, Rakshan. *Our Times* (Iran, 2002)
Farrokhzad, Forugh. *The House Is Black* (Iran, 1962)
Bendjelloul, Malik. *Searching for Sugar Man* (Sweden, 2012)
Godard, Jean-Luc. *Pravda* (France, 1970)
Godard, Jean-Luc. *See You at Mao* (France, 1970)
Godard, Jean-Luc. *Weekend* (France, 1967)
Kaufman, Jeff. *Nasrin* (USA, 2020)
Moore, Michael. *Michael Moore in Trumpland* (USA, 2016)
Naesi, Majed. *Inside the Iranian Uprising* (Great Britain, 2023)
Neshat, Shirin. *The Fury* (USA, 2023)
Neshat, Shirin. *Women Without Men* (USA, 2009)
Reichert, Julia and Jim Klein. *Growing Up Female* (USA, 1971)
Sarmiento, Valeria. *A Man When He Is a Man* (Chile, 1982)

Index

Note: Index is ordered word-by-word. Titles and references to images are in *italics*. All film works are made by Nahid Persson Sarvestani unless otherwise noted.

A Fatal Dress: Polygamy (Arslan, 2009), 56
A Man When He Is a Man (Sarmiento, 1982), 52
accented cinema, 4, 6, 27–30, 51, 63
　and *Queen and I, The* (2008), 27, 29, 37, 70, 76–7, 81, 83, 88, 97, 121, 149
　and *Seventeen Years of Longing* (1997), 5
accented feminism, 30
Adra, Najwa, 61
Afzali, Mahnaz, 11, 142
Aguayo, Angela J., 153–4
Ahmadi, Tania, 18–19
Ahmed, Leila, 20
Akbari, Mania, 15–16, 25, 42–3
Akbari, Mina, 14–15
Alinejad, Masih, 12, 38, 113–17, 119–20, 122, 124, 125–6, 134, 138, 146, 151–2, 155, 157–8

amateur, 115, 120
Andén-Papadopoulos, Kari, 157
Anders, Me and His 23 Other Women (2018), 32–3
　and first-person documentary, 32
apparatus, 4, 51, 107, 111, 124, 136, 141, 143, 158
authorial divestiture, 34–5, 91
　and *Be My Voice* (2021), 38–9, 113, 123–4, 155
　and Godard, Jean-Luc, 34–5
　and citizen-camera-witnessing videos, 108
　and *My Stolen Revolution* (2013), 38, 70, 91–2, 95, 102, 123
　and Persson Sarvestani, Nahid, 35, 104–6, 111, 159
　and *Son of a Mullah* (2023), 38–9, 137, 147
authorship, 34–5, 39, 69, 91–2

Index

and *Be My Voice* (2021), 118, 120, 123–4
and *Four Wives, One Man* (2007), 142
and Persson Sarvestani, Nahid, 31, 38–9, 64, 65, 70, 103–5, 123–4, 144, 146–7, 159
and *My Stolen Revolution* (2013), 86, 91–2, 144
and *Queen and I, The* (2008), 144
averted look, 22–3

Bauman, Zygmunt, 36, 74, 105
Be My Voice (2021), 12, 38, 109–10, 112, 113–24, *122*, 125–6, 129, 134. 138–9, 146, 151–2, 154–7, 159
and divested authorship, 123–4
and documentary apparatus, 118, 122, 139
and expository documentary, 117, 134, 146, 155
and first-person documentary, 38
and membrane, 113, 118, 121, 124
and observational documentary, 117, 155
and participatory documentary, 117–20
and veil, 114, 119, 151–2, 155
and vessel, 124
Bellour, Raymond, 83
Boussoualim, Malika, 21–2
Bruzzi, Stella, 72–3
Burton, Julianne, 46–7, 49–50

Chadwick, Andrew, 108
cinema interval, 93, 96–7, 101, 137
citizen-camera-witnessing videos, 108, 110, 157
consciousness-raising, 26–7, 51, 62, 64, 68, 100, 123, 159
and *Prostitution Behind the Veil* (2004), 50

divested authorship, 124
and *Be My Voice* (2021), 38, 123–4
and *My Stolen Revolution* (2013), 37, 141, 144–5
and Persson Sarvestani, Nahid, 35, 37–8, 69, 105, 159
and *Queen and I, The* (2008), 37, 144
and *Son of a Mullah* (2023), 38
Doane, Mary Ann, 57–8
documentation videos, 137
and *Be My Voice* (2021), 115, 119–20, 156–7
and *Son of a Mullah* (2023), 138
Dziga Vertov Group, 34–5, 124

enunciator, 5, 32, 37, 152–3, 156
and *Be My Voice* (2021), 124, 146, 152
and essay films, 67–9
and *My Stolen Revolution* (2013), 38, 86, 90, 92–6, 98, 101–5, 150
and *Queen and I, The* (2008), 72–5, 101–5
and *Son of a Mullah* (2023), 127, 136, 138, 145–6, 153

essay film, 31–4, 66–70, 102, 141, 145–6, 158
   and *Anders, Me and His 23 Other Women* (2018), 32–3
   and *Be My Voice* (2021), 138
   and *My Stolen Revolution* (2013), 37, 67–8, 70, 86, 90, 92, 98, 101–2, 104–5
   and *Queen and I, The* (2008), 37, 67–8, 70, 72, 74–8, 81–3, 97, 101–2, 104–5
   and *Prostitution Behind the Veil* (2004), 41
   and *Son of a Mullah* (2023), 138

Farah Pahlavi, 71–2, 74–84, 88, 91, 94, 103–4, 143, 149
Fish, Laura, 15
Fontini, Pinar, 30, 56
Formerly Youth Square (Mina Akbari, 2019), 14
Four Wives, One Man (2007), 2, 10, 31, 36, 41, 54–64, 57, 65, 96–7, 142, 148, 153
   and expository documentary, 31, 37, 41, 60, 64, 93, 142
   and observational documentary, 36
   and translation, 62
   and witness documentation, 56
Fury, The (Neshat, 2023), 16

gaze, 5, 16–17, 19, 22, 25, 29, 42
Gaines, Jane M., 110, 120, 136, 151, 155–8
Godard, Jean-Luc, 35, 92, 124
Growing Up Female (Reichert and Klein, 1971), 51

How Dare You Have Such a Rubbish Wish (Mania Akbari, 2022), 15–16, 25, 42–3
House Is Black, The (Farrokhzad, 1962), 10

Inside the Iranian Uprising (Naesi, 2023), 12–13
   and expository documentary, 159
   and veil, 12

Johnston, Claire, 64

Kaplan, E. A., 25
Kim, Jihoon, 107–11, 113, 115–16, 119–20, 136–9, 154, 157–8
Kuhn, Annette, 102

Ladies' Room, The (Afzali, 2003), 11, 142
   and expository documentary, 11
   and observational documentary, 11
Lebow, Alisa, 32, 34
Lesage, Julia, 26, 50–2
liquid authorship, 4, 35–6, 141
   and *Be My Voice* (2021), 158–9
   and *My Stolen Revolution* (2013), 91, 101, 103–5, 123, 145
   and *Queen and I, The* (2008), 74, 76, 83, 144
liquid enunciation, 83
liquid form, 74, 76
liquid modernity, 74, 105
looking, 24–5

membrane, 111
  and *Be My Voice* (2021), 113, 118, 121, 124
  and *Son of a Mullah* (2023), 125, 136, 139
meme, 120–1
  and *Be My Voice* (2021), 121
  and *My Stolen Revolution* (2013), 99
Merás, Lidia, 18, 94, 97
Metz, Christian, 98–9
Michael Moore in Trumpland (Moore, 2016), 66
Mina, An Xiao, 117, 121
mobilisation videos, 137, 154
  and *Be My Voice* (2021), 120, 157
Molony, Barbara, and Jennifer Nelson, 42
Mother of the Earth (Afzali, 2017), 14
Mulvey, Laura, 25, 42
My Mother, A Persian Princess (2000), 6–9, 19, 66, 141–2
  and enunciation, 6
  and observational documentary, 8
  and translation, 7
  and the veil, 7, 19
My Stolen Revolution (2013), 37–8, 65–7, 69–70, 84, 85–8, 90–2, 95, 98–9, 99, 101–5, 111, 119, 122–3, 141, 144–5, 151–2
  and enunciation, 86, 92, 98
  and expository documentary, 66, 68–9, 87, 91
  and first-person documentary, 37–8, 65–6, 68–9, 86, 95, 104–5, 146
  and participatory documentary, 141, 144
  and veil, 87, 96, 101, 151

Naficy, Hamid, 4–6, 22–3, 27–30, 37, 51, 63–4, 70, 76–7, 80–1, 97 149
Nasrin (Kaufman, 2020), 3
Nichols, Bill, 31, 46–7, 50, 60, 74, 117–18, 123
Neshat, Shirin, 15

on-the-ground, 111, 118, 125, 136–7, 155
online documentary practices, 107–11
Our Times (Bani-Etemad, 2002), 14

political mash-ups, 137
political mimesis (Gains), 110, 120, 125, 136, 155–8
Pollock, Griselda, 36
Poudeh, Reza, 10, 11, 62–3
Pravda (Godard et.al, 1970), 35
Profession: Documentarist (Abtahi et.al, 2014), 94
Prostitution Behind the Veil (2004), 1–2, 11, 23–5, 31, 36, 41, 43, 44–7, 49, 49–51, 53, 56–7, 60–1, 63–4, 65, 96, 128, 142, 148–9
  and expository documentary, 31, 37, 41, 47–8, 64, 93, 142
  and observational documentary, 25, 36, 47

Queen and I, The (2008), 27, 29, 37, 65–7, 69–70, 71–3, 76–7, 79, 80–4, 85, 88, 94–5, 97, 101, 104, 116, 121, 127, 143–4, 149, 153
and exilic denial, 27
and first-person documentary, 37, 65, 68–9, 72, 82–8, 104–5, 143
and expository documentary, 66, 68–9
and participatory documentary, 74

Rascaroli, Laura, 32, 37, 67–70, 72–4, 76, 82–3, 92, 96, 102–5, 144, 146, 158
Renov, Michael, 66–7, 110

Sabur, Abdus, 21
Sarmiento, Valeria, 51–2
Sayad, Cecilia, 34–5, 38–9, 69–70, 91–2, 104–6, 124
See You at Mao (Godard et.al, 1970), 34–5
Searching for Sugar Man (Bendjelloul, 2012), 66
Self-Health (Allen et.al., 1974), 51
Seventeen Years of Longing (1997), 5–6, 27–8
and exilic denial, 27
Shifman, Limor, 120–1
Silverman, Kaja, 35
Son of a Mullah (2023), 2, 38–9, 109, 122, 125–8, *130*, 133–9, *135*, 146, 147, 152, 154–5

and documentary apparatus, 139
and expository documentary, 128, 138, 146–7, 152
and first-person documentary, 38
and membrane, 125, 136, 139
and observational documentary, 128, 137
Suner, Asuman, 29–30

Trinh, T. Minh-Ha, 93, 95, 100–1, 140, 143–5, 147

Ulfsdotter, Boel, 70

Van de Peer, Stefanie, 5, 23–5, 57–8, 68
veil, 3, 5, 17, 19–23, 158

vernacular, 107, 111, 115, 139, 150
Weekend (Godard, 1967), 34
White, Patricia, 63–4
witness, 31, 56, 86–7, 91, 107, 109, 120, 145
witness documentation, 31, 107, 109, 111, 115, 137, 139
and *Be My Voice* (2021), 115, 118–20, 156–7
and *Inside the Iranian Uprising* (Naesi, 2023), 12–13
and *My Stolen Revolution* (2013), 86–8, 91–2, 145
and *Queen and I, The* (2008), 80, 85–8, 90–2
and *Son of a Mullah* (2023), 138

Women of the Revolution (Mina Akbari, work in progress), 14–15

Women Without Men (Neshat, 2009), 16

Yu, Kiki Tianqi, 37

Yacavone, Daniel, 98, 100, 122–3

Zimmermann, Patricia R., 110–11, 113, 118, 123–4, 136, 146

EU representative:
Easy Access System Europe
Mustamäe tee 50, 10621 Tallinn, Estonia
Gpsr.requests@easproject.com

www.ingramcontent.com/pod-product-compliance
Lightning Source LLC
Chambersburg PA
CBHW071425160426
43195CB00013B/1816